BELONG

A GOD-GIVEN BLUEPRINT TO CONTINUALLY REACH THE LOST AND DISCIPLE NEW BELIEVERS

BY

CHRIS DONALD

33rd Company
United States of America

For questions or permission requests, chris@33rdcompany.org

ISBN 979-8-9873986-0-9 (pbk)
ISBN 979-8-9873986-1-6 (ebk)

Printed in the United States of America

Evangelism and discipleship was never meant to be divorced but was intended by Jesus for every Christian. Throughout the ages somehow The Great Commission has become the great suggestion. Chris reminds us in Belong that these go hand in hand and shares practical testimonies of the fruit of salvation working in individuals lives.

I personally had Chris come to one of our outreach events for the purpose of training and equipping people in spreading the gospel. Chris equipped people to pray for the lost before they ever went out, and some of the individuals there said it was one of the most powerful equipping times for evangelism that they've ever experienced.

Chris is an evangelist who, in the last few years, has seen God Move on people's lives through Belong. My prayer is that God would light a fire in your heart and that you too would start a discipleship gathering that is based around relationship with Jesus first and then to His people.

May you become effective in sharing your faith and making disciples that make disciples. Whatever you learn from Belong, I hope you look for ways to apply it in your own life and dive deep into the word of God to discover that evangelism and discipleship are still in the heart of God, and that eternity is real.

- Chris Overstreet, *Compassion to Action*

This book by Chris Donald to equip Christians to preach the gospel, and to equip churches to consistently make disciples is refreshingly simple, essentially needed, and wonderfully inspiring. This book will challenge you, encourage you, and equip you to live like Jesus to be a part of the Great Commission. As a close friend of Chris, and as a senior pastor of a local church, I can tell you first hand that Chris truly lives out this message every day. This approach is Scripturally based, engages the local church body effectively, and has shown consistent and tangible fruit. The fruit is seen in souls finding salvation, in people being discipled, in those disciples preaching the gospel and being added to the local church, and in the local church people personally growing as they engage in the original call that Jesus gave His church. I highly endorse and recommend this book, Belong, and the entire ministry of 33rd Company.

- Jonathan Christopherson, *Senior Pastor, The Promise Church*

Chris embodies his message. If you were to spend time with him, you would experience discipleship in everyday life. You would, first and foremost, feel loved and valued; you would have fun; you would see him share about Jesus a dozen times in a very casual way; you would spend time in long passionate prayer, and then you would enjoy joyful laughs. All of this, in a very non-religious way, that is under the easy and light yoke of Christ.

Reading this book is like getting to spend a week with Chris hearing his heart, his philosophy of ministry, what drives him, and why it drives him so. As humans we are subject to the limitations of our humanity. Many will not get a chance to spend a week with Chris in person, but reading this book is like getting to look into his heart and soul — poured out on pages that will inspire you, convict you, move you, and effectively equip you to do the work of an evangelist who makes disciples in everyday life.

- Richie Nelson, *Senior Pastor, Deeper Church*

Not many people can write a book that makes winning and discipling the lost look easy. But that's exactly what Chris Donald has done in this practical, effective, life changing book. This isn't just another book about making disciples or sharing your faith; it's a blueprint anyone or any church can follow and see Kingdom results. Most Pastors only dream of having a vibrant, growing, life changing outreach and discipleship ministry in their church. I have seen that dream become a reality. Chris and his team came to our church and started with a desire to reach our city and train our people to sustain a move of God. That is exactly what happened. What started with just one person in a living room turned into a weekly revival in our church lobby. People were born again, delivered, water baptized and filled with the Spirit every single week. Even long after Chris and his team have left, that revival is still going on because the tools in this book work. If you're a pastor or leader looking to see the lost saved and discipled in your area, this is the book for you!

- Stephen Holley, *Senior Pastor, Generation Church*

A SPECIAL THANK YOU

I want to thank a few people that have impacted my life greatly as I have grown in the things of God. I would not be where I am today without the love, support and prayers of many people that I don't have the room in this book to fully thank but if you're reading this and you have been in my life and have helped to guide me, thank you.

Mom and Dad, thank you for trusting God and letting me run after him with all my heart. I Love you both and am so thankful that you have always supported me on this crazy, wild and fun journey!

Patty Donald, thank you for being an aunt that has taught me who the Holy Spirit is and what it means to pursue the Kingdom with all that I have. The years that you have poured into me and the phone calls that you have answered when I was in a spiritual battle served as a life line to heaven for me and my family. Thank you!

Aaron Christopherson, Thank you for being a friend that pushed and sometimes pulled me forward. When I didn't believe and I didnt see what God had next you always encouraged me to move forward and to believe God for great things. It's not possible to be where I am today without your friendship and love. You are a true gift to me and I am so thankful that we get to advance God's Kingdom together. Thank you!

Stephen Holley, Thank you for standing with me and being a true friend in the midst of crazy spiritual warfare. This book was written right after the six months I spent with you in Florida and we both know that the devil was trying to stop Belong from ever coming alive. Thank you for putting friendship before ministry! Thank you for taking a stand with Chelsea and I. Please know that you will always have a friend that will go to war with you! Thank you!

Scott McNamara, Thank you for your friendship and for being a big brother in my life. You were an answer to prayer in my life. I wanted to be a more fruitful evangelist and God sent you to teach me what it means to be a reaping evangelist who fights for souls. You are one of the most impactful people in my life. Your life has truly marked me and I am so thankful for what I learned from you. I love you and I am so thankful for you and Jesus at The Door. Thank you!

Jerry Wilbur, Thank you for believing in me and spending time with me at Luckman's Coffee. I always look forward to spending time with you. Your heart to see the lost come to know Jesus is so pure and real. Thank you for taking this book from a word document to an actual, physical book. Thank you for investing in me and the work that God has given me to steward over the years. I believe that this book will impact many people over the years to come and you are a part of that. Thank you!

Brian Ripp, Thank you for designing the cover. It's one of a kind and better than I could have imagined it being. But most importantly, thank you for making disciples with me in Texas. The best is yet to come!

Kristie Dunnigan, I can't thank you enough for the hours that you have spent editing this book. I know it was a lot of work because I can't spell and my grammar is terrible. You took a messy passionate letter to the church and turned it into a book. Thank you!

Lavonne Hira, You're in heaven! But this thank you section would not be complete without saying thank you for the years that you have poured into my life. I have the button and I am going to run this race well. I will see you in heaven soon. I will not forget that, "All things are in Christ, so help yourself."

P.S. Please tell Jesus hi for me!

DEDICATION

I want to dedicate this book to my best friend
Chelsea Donald. You are the best wife
a man could ever ask for.

You have believed in the words that God has spoken
and you have said "Yes" from the beginning. You have
put the call above everything else in life and your "Yes" is
changing the world. I love you, Chelsea. Thank you for
putting His kingdom before your comfort. You are the best
gift God has ever given me. The best is yet to come!

FOREWORD

"Hey Tom, I gotta tell you what the Lord showed me last night!"

I still remember those words the day Chris walked into the green room at Lifestyle Christianity. As he sat down and began to tell me this "plan," this "strategy" the Lord had given him, I was overwhelmed.

"This is God!" I responded. I knew it in my spirit. And I was excited. For him and for the millions this plan would help usher into the Kingdom of God.

That plan Chris shared that day in the green room...that simple yet crazy, amazing plan...that was Belong!

This causes me to think of other "plans" God has given to men and women of God throughout centuries. For example, a man named Bill Bright was given a simple plan for sharing the gospel. He wrote it in a tract called, "The Four Spiritual Laws." One day in November in 1978 at the University of North Carolina, a man named Carl Broggi shared that one simple tract with a 19-year-old Varsity Tennis player. The truth in that simple gospel presentation pierced that young man's heart and, in that moment, he was changed forever. That man was me. I was one of hundreds of thousands, if not millions, that were changed by one simple plan given to one humble man.

Simple plans can change people. They can change cities. They can change nations. And I say watch out world... because Belong is about to bring in another huge harvest!

Let me tell you specifically why I believe the revelation held within the pages of this book is about to be used by God in mighty and incredible ways...

I personally know the power of how simple, caring discipleship can keep a new believer from falling back into the world. After I came to Jesus, Carl poured into me for weeks and months. I looked forward to our times together reading the Word of God and talking about the Scriptures. Carl would take me with him to share the gospel and it was only natural for me to begin to imitate. In a short period of time, I had led many to Jesus at UNC Chapel Hill and, at one point, I was leading 3 different bible studies and discipling close to 25 others in the same manner Carl had discipled and invested into me!

I saw and experienced firsthand the difference one-to-one discipleship made on my life and that of others, and I simultaneously saw how new believers who were simply encouraged to "go to church" often didn't make it in their spiritual walk with Jesus.

Don't get me wrong...I love church services. Over the years, however, even as a pastor leading hundreds of services, I have seen the limitations of them. Great teaching happens in many of them. The making of and multiplying disciples happens in hardly any of them.

Jesus said, "Go and make disciples." The command is clear, so why is it so rare? There is a reason for this.

I don't blame pastors for what DOESN'T happen within a Sunday service. The dynamics of large group meetings are designed to accomplish other objectives. In order to accomplish true discipleship, however, there must be additional factors besides teaching and worship. There must be...hmm...how do I say it. I'm afraid if I just use one of the particular words I am thinking about, it may not sink in. And it must sink in! We are desperately missing this in most congregations! Let me approach it this way:

In the great commission, Jesus said (and I am almost quoting here) - All authority in heaven and on earth has been given to me. Therefore go and make disciples of all nations, baptizing them in the name of the Father and of the Son and of the Holy Spirit, and teaching them everything I have commanded you. And surely I am with you always, to the very end of the age.

Have you read that verse before? Well, if you have, you may realize that I left out two words..."to obey."

Jesus did not say "and teaching them everything I have commanded you." He said "and teaching them to obey everything I have commanded you."

In today's churches regarding the area of evangelism and discipleship, there is much teaching happening...but there is little "teaching to obey." Teaching to obey is almost impossible to accomplish in a large group setting alone because it is something that must be modeled. We must model it. We must show others how to do it and how to live it. We must be the example and then say, "now you try it!"

Personally, I like to call this process activation. Activation is helping someone do what they want to do, but don't quite know how to get there...and well, Belong gets you there! That's why this book exists, and when applied, I think you're going to be in awe.

In 2019 when I heard Chris share this amazingly simple multiplication strategy, I knew instantly: Belong is a missing piece to help Christians and congregations to DO what they really want to do - evangelism and discipleship. I wish these two things, two of the most basic things that Jesus told us to do, hadn't gotten lost in our Christian activities...but they did and they have. So, let's go back...let's go back 2000 years. Because it is so simple! And without going back to the simplicity of what Jesus told us to do, without the simplicity of what God gave Chris within these pages, we are missing out on exponential increase.

Souls need to be saved, delivered, and set free. Souls are depending upon our activation. Without it, we are missing out on the privilege of watching those who are lost and don't know who they are grow into soldiers for the King of Kings. We are missing out on the multiplication that exists on the other side of our decision to obey.

Trying to medicate ourselves with another good service or another hyped-up emotional high is not going to do it. It's time for the fruit that lasts! It's time for the laborers to respond and to get to work in the fields God's invited us into. After all, the harvest is promised to be plentiful!

Tom Ruotolo
Founder of City Quake

CONTENTS

SECTION 1:
INTRO AND HEART OF BELONG

At the time of writing this, I'm sitting in a coffee shop in Bend, Oregon taking time to get away, slow down, and reflect on all that God has done over the past few years in my life and ministry. It has been a wild couple of years full of many ups and downs along the way. Throughout this past season, one thing has kept me going. Day after day, one thing has kept me moving forward: What Jesus has called us to do as born again believers here on this earth.

Jesus was clear when He said, "Go and make disciples of all nations."

I know that we as Christians know this famous passage of scripture and many of us can even quote it if asked, but my question for you is this: Do you live it? Do you walk it out? Do you live to honor God by doing what he has told us to do?

To me, this is not something that He asks us to do if we want to or feel like it. It is something that Jesus has commanded us to do in His word. I know that we all like the soft and cuddly Jesus who loves us for who we are and don't get me wrong, I love Jesus and he loves me too, but I believe that is why I am so serious about the call that He has put before us that we may fulfill. The call takes work, it takes effort, it takes drive and it takes passion. It takes real perseverance. It demands real grit.

I believe that the church has lost much of its grit in the west. I believe that the church has become weak and lifeless because it has put aside the great commission. Or perhaps the church has convinced itself The Great Commission is being fulfilled by having a Sunday morning church service. I'm for Sunday morning church services and great worship teams but what I'm not for is having good programs while failing to reach the lost and make disciples. Remember, religion is a form of godliness void of the power of God. Unfortunately, many churches in the west have a form of religion without power. Sadly, The Holy Spirit could never show up and many churches would still be able to have their church service as normal!

As I'm here reflecting on the past few years since God spoke to me in the night through a vision, I am seeing more clearly than ever the need to get back to the basics of what He has called us to.

I want to share with you what God spoke to me. I want to let you in on the secret to His heart, which really isn't a secret at all; it's quite clear in the Bible what pleases Him and what He wants from us. My desire is to encourage you, and hopefully, to motivate you to step out and truly begin to fulfill the great commission. Before I do, however, I want to pause and take a moment to talk about where your heart needs to be before jumping into this: You need to be open to change. You need to be open to being wrong in some areas. You need to be open to feeling the conviction of the Holy Spirit. You need to be open to change and to doing things differently as He leads you.

What I want you to understand is that God doesn't anoint a plan, He anoints sons and daughters. The reason why the plan that God gave me works is because He is working in and through my life daily as His son. I have surrendered my life fully to Him and I have said yes to the call. We can have the best plan without the right heart and it will fail. We can have the worst plan with a great heart and it will succeed and bear fruit. I don't want you to read this and think, "If I do this program or plan I will see fruit just like Chris and his team." That is not the case. You will see fruit when you are obedient to the call of God on your life as a born again believer.

Since the moment Jesus called the first disciples, the original call has never changed. We have changed the call with our religion and our excuses, but Jesus has not changed one bit. Jesus said, "Follow me and I will make you fishers of men." Why? Because He was, and still is, a fisher of men. In Luke 19:10 Jesus says, "I came to seek and to save the lost." This is who Jesus is. He came to seek and to save. That has not changed one bit.

Jesus didn't say follow me to a university and I will teach you how to fish for men. He said follow me and watch me fish for men, and then understand that you are called to the same thing. If you call yourself a follower of Jesus, it is important that you understand you are called to fish for men because Jesus desires that all men shall come to know Him. This call has so overtaken me that, at times, it wakes me up at night. I begin to wonder if I'm going crazy but then I read the words of Jesus once again and I remember the call has not changed. I remember that wherever I find myself today, I am invited to be a part of that call.

So before you go any further in this book, I want to encourage you to pause and ask yourself, "Am I willing to count the cost?" Because there is a call, and with that call comes a cost.

Take a moment and really ask yourself, "Am I willing to count the cost to make disciples?" I say it all the time - it doesn't cost us our lives to go to church but it will cost us our lives to make disciples. It often doesn't cost us our lives to preach the gospel but it will cost us our lives to make disciples. What I mean in saying this is, it doesn't cost you your life to just preach the gospel. With discipleship, you are committing your life to people and to the process, just as Jesus did, and it will demand your life.

Sure, it costs something to share our faith but let's be honest for a moment: We could go on outreach for 2 hours, share the gospel with 50 people, and then go home and binge-watch Netflix doing nothing to steward the people that we spoke to on outreach. That is not the work of making disciples. To commit to people and to the process of discipleship is costly, and it is the call given to each of us. And that is the question you need to ask yourself, "Am I willing?"

THE NET

Let me tell you a story to paint a picture for you about the cost of discipleship. The reality is that many, if not most of the people that will read this, will have at some point in their Christian walk shared their faith and may have even gone on outreach. I want to show you that there is more that we can do to begin to see the people that we meet truly get discipled and plugged into the local church.

One day, I was on outreach in Saint Petersburg, Florida where my family lived for 6 months when God led us to a man in a way that was truly supernatural. Before going out, we prayed. As we prayed, we felt the Lord speak to us to go to a boat dock near a seafood restaurant, and oddly enough, we kept hearing the word "Elbow." We looked on the map to find there was a boat dock right next to a place called "The "Devil's Elbow" (This was a real place on the map!), and it just so happened there was also a seafood restaurant in the parking lot.

When we arrived, I jumped out of the car and ran up to a man named Rashad moments before he walked into the restaurant to begin work. I said, "Hey man, I know this may appear crazy but we prayed and God led us to you. Can I share the Gospel with you?" He said yes (You'll be surprised how open and willing people are if you just step out and ask!). I preached the Gospel and he gave his life to Jesus right there. It was amazing. And that moment, our work is not over. In fact, it's only just beginning.

I reached out to him for six weeks with little to no response. After six weeks, he finally made it to church and had a powerful encounter with God. Following that encounter, I continued following up week-after-week. After a few weeks of persistence, he came a second time where he encountered God again in a powerful way, and his schedule opened up to allow him to come to Belong where he got water baptized and filled with the Holy Spirit. Today, he is plugged into the local church, growing in his faith, and doing well!

I tell that story because it was a journey of not only being submitted to God and His leading, but being committed to the process and the person in order to get them connected to God. Yes, he was born again in a moment, but he needed discipleship and a church family around him to get to where he needed to be in God. It required commitment, persistence, and time.

At the time, he couldn't drive and it required being inconvenienced in order to ensure he had transportation. It reminds me of something we say often: Discipleship is not glamorous but it is glorious. It requires hard work but I like that because when I think of the words of Jesus in Luke 10:2, He says "The Labors are few." God is not looking for celebrity Christians, He is looking for laborers.

So what is it that God said to me? Okay, here it is:
"If you create a net, I will fill it."

As He spoke that to me in a dream, I saw a coffee shop area at the ministry school where I was pastoring at the time filled with about 100 people, and half of them I knew were new believers. When I woke up from the vision, I knew exactly what God meant by creating a net and Him filling it. What He was saying to me was, "If you create time and space and take me at my word, I will fill that time and space with new believers."

Following that encounter, I took inventory of my personal time and schedule and realized that I had no time set aside in my schedule to disciple new believers. I'm very specific when I say "new" believers because if I'm honest, I believe we as the church have turned discipleship into discipling believers only. A lot of our church growth, at least in America, is church transfers. That's okay from time to time but I want to see a movement of God where people are born again, discipled, and added to the church daily (I think that's what you want to see as well since you are reading this book!).

When I looked at my schedule, I saw that I had no time for the call Jesus gave to us all and that something needed to change. I talked to my wife, Chelsea, and we decided that we would count the cost and together respond to what God had said before we ever talked about it with others. It would be easy to have a great idea and start preaching about it without living it out, but that would mean sharing good theories, not real strategies from heaven that have been tried and tested.

Ever since the moment I heard from the Lord, I started walking out his instructions. Leaders often told me I needed to get this out to share with other leaders, and while I knew that was right, I first needed to walk it out myself so what

I was giving was more than a theory. I wanted to be able to say, "I have done this and it works." At the time of writing this, I have personally started four Belongs. The first was in Texas, then Florida, Washington State and now back in Texas again at our new home church Mercy Culture. It works. Why does it work? Because it was God's idea.

It all began with my wife and I simply deciding to set aside Tuesday nights at 6:30 PM. Time that would be used to invite new believers into our home. It was that simple. The first week we ever had Belong we had James at our house. It then quickly grew to eight new believers in my home weekly in a very short amount of time. When I set aside the time to create a net, God filled it. Exactly what He said He'd do. I even began to find that as I went around the city with a net that I created for God to fill, I would find people that had that specific time open in their schedule.

One day, I was walking into LA Fitness in Fort Worth, Texas and saw a man named Florin sitting by the entrance to the men's locker room. I simply asked if I could share the gospel with him, and two hours later, he was born again. I missed my workout that day but Florin was saved that day. I then asked him if he wanted to come to my house for Belong on Tuesday night at 6:30 PM, he responded by sharing that it was the only night of the week that he was free to do anything. I was amazed that in a city so large, I would run into a man that was not only ready for the gospel but free only on Tuesday night to come to my house to be discipled. He came the next day and we read Galatians 3 together with the group. This testimony marked me personally. It displayed to me the intricacy and faithfulness of God, and it displayed the heart of Jesus to draw all men unto Himself.

From that point, Belong continued to grow in my home. My wife and I then decided that since it worked at our house, that we would move it to the cafe at Lifestyle Christiantiy University (LCU), where I was pastoring. At that time, LCU had about 350 students that went out on outreach twice a week. I intentionally equipped the students to be people who didn't just share their faith but to be people who made disciples.

Moving Belong to the school's cafe enabled every student to have a "net" to invite people from outreach to, and I encouraged and equipped them in creating their own nets if the allotted time in the cafe did not work for those they were ministering to. The students got it quickly. We have countless testimonies of people coming to Belong, getting saved, water baptized, and filled with the Holy Spirit. It took off like a wildfire. Before we knew it, one night in an incredibly large cafe could no longer accommodate everyone. We then had Belong happening twice a week with weekly salvations, water baptisms, and people receiving the Holy Spirit and speaking in tongues. What we saw was a true book of Acts move of God.

At that point, I knew we had something that worked and was effective. It was never meant to be a program. Discipleship is not a program, it's a family. And that's what it became. Belong became a family where people of all backgrounds were welcomed in, invited to encounter God, and to be born again.

Before long, people began to hear about what was happening. Some leaders and others gave feedback that it was awesome but that it was happening because it was attached to LCU and because there was an army of students being sent out. If I'm honest, even though the majority of the work was done by a small, committed group of people, I too thought that being at LCU had its advantages to being at a local church. So we decided to head to Generation Church in Largo, Florida, and attempt to do it again. And it happened again.

We saw the same fruit that happened at LCU happen at a local church. Within 6 months, it was explosive. We watched as Belong grew from one home with one person (just like Texas' beginning), to a church lobby filled with salvations, water baptisms, and people being baptized in the Holy Spirit weekly. We truly witnessed a move of God that is still happening to this day!

Just yesterday, I received a message that three people were born again during the Belong outreach, two were saved at the Belong gathering, and four people were water baptized and filled with the Holy Spirit last night.

These stories have brought me the confidence to know that if a group of people agree to run after the great commission, then they will be successful with or without me. I believe that if we simply believe and obey what Jesus has called us to do, we will see people won to the Lord and discipled.

So as I'm sitting here in Bend, reflecting on the past two years of what occurred when I was simply obedient to believe Jesus at his word. I'm asking myself what it was that made this work successful. Why did it work for me but it doesn't seem to work for others who try similar things?

On the following pages, I'm going to take a moment to give you my honest, raw, gut opinion as to why I believe I have been successful. This is what you could call "The secret sauce" to the Belong strategy. I want you to know this: I don't really care if you ever start a Belong or anything that resembles one. That's not why I've poured my heart into sharing everything I can and writing this. I care about you fulfilling the great commission and honoring God. So if you don't read anything beyond this next section, get this section. I believe it is the secret to the success of Belong thus far and I believe if you take these thoughts and principles and apply them to your life, you will change the world one person at a time and fulfill the great commission.

BELIEVE YOU ARE CALLED TO MAKE DISCIPLES

There are so many religious lies out there that stop people from stepping into the fullness of what God has called them to as a believer. Lies like "I'm not gifted" or "I'm not called to be a street evangelist."

Listen, if you are a believer and you don't think that you are naturally gifted in that way I want to share something with you: You may not think that you are gifted but you have been gifted the greatest gift of all which is the gift of The Holy

Spirit. The gift of the Holy Spirit is the greatest evangelist in the world. If you have Him, you are gifted and can share your faith at a gas pump or in a supermarket or anywhere you plant your feet. You need to believe you are called because if you are a Christian, you are called.

I want to encourage you to read the book of Acts and understand this: it is a playbook, not a history book. Understand that you have been invited into the greatest story of all time and that you are called to be a key player.

You are called by God to make disciples. Stop believing any lie that would tell you otherwise.

PERSONAL PRAYER TIME AS A NON-NEGOTIABLE

Having a personal prayer life is not an option for me. Connecting with God is the most important thing that I do in my life. If I don't pray, I don't fully come to life and I could never share with the world a Jesus that I don't encounter daily. To me, sharing my faith is not about sharing information about God with people; it's about sharing with people a God that I encountered and continue to encounter daily.

We must remember that we are witnesses. We don't witness only when we go on outreach, our life is a witness to all those that are around us whether we are on fire or not. I want to encourage you to pray and to pray daily. Jesus said in Matthew 6:6, "But when you pray, go into your room and shut the door and pray to your Father who is in secret. And your Father who sees in secret will reward you." Jesus didn't say if you pray, He said when you pray. As a Christian, prayer is not an option, it's a way of life. We also see in this scripture that Jesus says that the father who sees in secret will reward openly. The way I read this is: No prayer, no reward. What is the reward? The reward is time with Him and being in His presence. The reward is God's power being on your life so that others will come to know Him through you.

Take time and begin to pray daily and remember, God doesn't think in time he thinks of connection. If you have 10 minutes to pray, then pray for ten minutes before you go to work. If you have two hours to pray, then pray for two hours. The most important thing is that you connect with God daily so that you have an overflow to give away to others. We cannot give away what we do not have.

LIVING EVERYDAY ON MISSION AS A FULL-TIME CHRISTIAN

Why is it that when people go on mission trips they seem to catch on fire and see God do so many different things, including miracles? Why do people say things like "God works miracles in Africa but not in the USA"?

I believe it's because when a person goes on a mission trip they have faith and expectancy for God to move, so He moves. What if we lived with that level of expectancy in our cities and towns daily? I wake up every morning and treat each day like I'm on a mission trip. I call it being a full-time Christian. When you begin to live on mission every day of your life, it is the most exciting way you could possibly live. You will begin to see God move everywhere that you go. We are not waiting on a move of God, God is waiting on us to move and be obedient with the gospel that He has given us to share with the world.

I believe that prayers go up and that God is looking for people to carry those prayers out. When I walk out of the house in the morning I look up and say, "I'm ready," knowing that God is going to line up assignment after assignment for me to do for Him that day. I can't tell you enough how fun it is to live this way. Multiple times, I have found myself talking to a couple at the grocery store, the wife is a believer and the husband is hardened to the gospel, and as I begin to share I can see the wife looking at me and saying, "Don't stop, I have been praying for you and God sent you to me to share with my husband."

One time I was in the Philippines at the airport and I began to talk to a Chinese man that was there on business. He shared with me that his wife was a believer and that he was not, so I asked him if his wife had been praying for him, to which he said, "Yes." I told him that his wife had prayed me into that moment to tell him about Jesus. He was born again that day and got on the plane to head back to his saved wife as a saved man with a new heart.

I want to encourage you to begin to live on mission because you will begin to see lives changed simply living as a full-time Christian. And as a full-time Christian, your mission is where your feet are.

CREATING A NET FOR GOD TO FILL

When God spoke to me to create a net and that he would fill it, it truly changed everything when it came to effectiveness and seeing people make the transition from an outreach encounter to actually coming and desiring to be discipled. When I counted the cost and created a net, specifically for new believers, what happened was profound. God began to send me to people that were ready for the gospel and ready to be discipled. I couldn't believe that I never thought of it before because it was such a simple concept. That's why I love it so much. It is simple and anybody can do it. I want to encourage you, if you are reading this, simply create a space for discipleship in your schedule and then step out and begin to share with people. I believe God will quickly fill your net.

There are so many people in your city ready for Jesus but are you ready for them?

One day our team went on outreach for about an hour and decided to go by an apartment building. Jonnie, our intern, and another team member knocked on a door and a man named Tyrell opened the door. Tyrell had found Jesus on his own a month prior to our team knocking on his door and was born again alone in his house, and had been praying and fasting on his own with no other believers or church family. And God led us to his door. That night he came to Belong, was encouraged in community, and was water baptized.

Why does this kind of stuff happen? Because God is looking for people and churches that will take care of his new believers and help them to grow up in God. If you create a net, God will fill it.

Many that are reading this have tried many other things and are tired but I want to remind you of the time that Jesus said to the men who fished all night, "Cast your net on the other side of the boat." They replied, "At your word Lord," and they brought in a large catch of fish. They cast the net, Jesus provided the fish. You have to have a net to cast. Once you have it, cast it out. God will provide the fish.

BEING SOLD OUT, NO MATTER WHAT

A few months ago, my wife and I were driving, and I looked at her with tears in my eyes and shared that if I never lead another person to the Lord again for the rest of my life I still wouldn't stop sharing my faith. This thought came from two things I had been thinking about. The first reason is this: Jesus saved me and completely transformed my life. I have to share with others what happened to me so they may have the same experience. The second reason is this: Jesus told me what to do and I want to be an obedient son and follower of Jesus.

Oftentimes, when we don't see success we're tempted to stop or shift our focus. I want to encourage you to remember your testimony and all that Jesus has done for you. I want to encourage you to keep the words of Jesus before you, and to possess the attitude that you will not stop for any reason. Of the first disciples, all but one died following Jesus while carrying out the great commission. If there is anything worth living for, this is it. If there is anything worth dying for, this is it. It's time to take the words of Jesus seriously and go for it with no plan B. Consistency and commitment will change the world if you simply put your hand to the plow and have no other options. If you do that, I believe you will be successful.

I tell our teams all the time that success is doing what Jesus has called us to do, which is attempting to make disciples. If you are going out there and going for that one goal, just your act of obedience is a success. Decide today to be committed and consistent and just see what will happen a year from now. For a while, people thought, "Oh that's cool what Chris and his team are doing at Belong, a few people got saved and are being discipled," but when it kept happening week after week and began to pick up momentum that never stopped, all of a sudden people started calling me. People wanted to know what was happening and they wanted to know why.

The answer is simple: Consistency.

Consistency over time bears great fruit. You may see 25 people saved at Easter or Christmas once a year at church but what happens when you see 10 people saved a week? That's 520 people in a year. That's bigger than most churches.

What I'm saying is this: Stay consistent and faithful and you will see big things over time.

KEEPING THE FOCUS ON THE ONE

It's all about the one. For Jesus, it always has been. For us, it always needs to be. The moment that we begin to get our eyes off the one and onto the size of the crowd, we will get off track. Jesus left the 99 for the one. Don't get me wrong, I'm all about big churches but they need to be big and about the one. Jesus was amazing in that he could be in a crowd and see the one over and over again.

I was recently at a restaurant and they gave me a table number so they could bring the food out to me. The number was 99, to which I said, "Hey that's one of my favorite numbers!" The man behind the counter asked me why and I said, "because Jesus left the 99 for the one and I believe that you are the one he is coming after today!" I shared the gospel with him and he was born again right there at the counter.

Multiple times at our Belong gatherings the whole night would seem to be about one person that showed up that night. We train our team to see the one and not the crowd. If there is a crowd, that's okay, we just want to have eyes to see the individual that came and needs an encounter with God. We cannot lose that because Jesus never will.

One night a man came to Belong in Texas, and as we were in worship, I received a word of knowledge about somebody having a deaf ear. I took a moment to share and a man that had come for the first time raised his hand and said that it was him. As we prayed for him, his ear was healed and he powerfully encountered the presence of God. As the night went on, we had a moment for people to respond to the Gospel and he quickly stood up to be born again. Because of what God had done for him he was ready to be saved. We then moved into a time of baptism and he was ready to be water baptized and came out of the water baptized in the Holy Spirit. Why am I telling this story? Because that night it seemed like the whole gathering was orchestrated just for him. It was centered around what he needed in order to be introduced to Jesus, because that's what Jesus does. He goes after and knows exactly how to pursue the one.

We would see this night after night, and our team celebrates one salvation like there are 15,000 saved because we are simply not moved by numbers, we are moved by the one. We pray and believe for crowds because we are able to see the one and their needs in the midst of the crowd. Holding this heart is important because it's the heart of Jesus.

Some people are against big churches. I am not. I want really big churches! I actually believe if there is a person in your town that is unsaved then your church is too small. I just want to make sure that no matter how big, my focus always stays on the one.

TRAINING AND EQUIPPING OTHERS TO LEAD BESIDE YOU

We are called to fulfill the great commission as the family of God. Just imagine for a moment what would be accomplished with each and every person bringing their specific gift to the table. One of the sad things about the western church, or more specifically the church in the US, is many in the church think they are just supposed to show up, watch the pastor, and hopefully leave changed. Oftentimes, we think it's the pastor's job to fix, help, and to minister to us as people in the church. This idea that has come into the church has actually crippled the church and caused it to become a consumer-driven culture, not a kingdom culture.

In Ephesians 4:11-12, it says "and he gave the apostles, the prophets, the evangelists, the shepherds, and teachers, to equip the saints for the work of ministry, for building up the body of Christ." The five-fold ministry is meant to equip every believer to do the work of the ministry. Now, I know that many have heard this before and even at this moment are saying, "Yeah, that's right!" But I want to ask you a serious question: If you believe this theology, are you actually walking it out in your life? If not, I want to challenge you to begin to be equipped and to step out and do something with it.

The other thing that happens in our western context is that many of the five-fold leaders in the body of Christ don't empower and equip people because they like being the only one to do something. Perhaps it's the attention, a feeling of significance and importance, or a blend of both but in doing so they have become what I like to call celebrity Christians: Christian's that work to build their kingdom, not God's Kingdom.

So how do you know if you are falling into that trap of insecurity and competition that would stop you from equipping others? There is a pretty simple litmus test to see if this is happening in your ministry, and it's this: If you were removed from your church or ministry tomorrow, would it continue on?

I understand that it would be different and there would need to be some adjusting but what I'm saying is, if you didn't show up to your church or ministry tomorrow, would the doors stay open? Would there still be Kingdom impact? If the answer is no, then I would encourage you to begin to find people that you can pass responsibility off to and begin to equip and raise up.

At some churches, if the main pastor is not preaching, people don't show up. I understand that some people have a high gift on their life and their gifting draws people but I would pose the question: Is that ministry built on man or on God? We need to lead like we're leaving. We need to raise up men and women to step into responsibility. We need to lead so when we're gone, the work continues.

To date, I have started three Belongs and at the point of this writing, I am in the process of starting another. Upon leaving the previous Belongs, they have continued to bear fruit. This is because I found people to equip, give responsibility to, and raise up. They were equipped and championed to take it and run. Paul says to Timothy in 2 Timothy 2:2, "and what you have heard from me in the presence of many witnesses entrust to faithful men, who will be able to teach others also."

We must be leaders that equip and release others to run faster and further than us. Insecurity and the need for recognition is death to Kingdom activity, so remember this: Anything built on self in the Kingdom of God will self-destruct!

BECOMING AND REMAINING A GRITTY CHRISTIAN

A few years ago, my wife and I had a miscarriage that was very difficult to walk through. The night it happened I was leading a School of Evangelism in the Northwest. Chelsea called me and asked if I could meet her at the emergency room. At this time, we didn't know what was happening but Chelsea felt off. When I got to the emergency room waiting area I hugged Chelsea and prayed for her, and then I began to share the gospel with everyone in the waiting room. I decided that if the devil is going to send me and my wife to the emergency room, I'm going to make him pay the price.

Later that night when we got home, Chelsea lost baby "Mercy." It was very difficult. We were processing many different emotions and thoughts coming at us. The next morning was the second morning of the School of Evangelism. Many of my friends and peers told me to stay home and be with Chelsea, which I absolutely would have done if that's what she wanted. I will never forget what my wife did, however, as she looked at me and said "Go to work and tell as many people about Jesus as you possibly can."

I went to work that day and equipped people to go on outreach. I went out that day and people heard the gospel, were physically healed, and multiple people got saved. What if I stayed home? What if I didn't go? I can hear the voice of reason saying, "You need to slow down and be careful," and that may be true but I'm sharing with you what makes us effective: We don't stop. When we get hit, we hit back and slug it out. As believers, we are built for war and will not back down at any fight because Jesus is King and King Jesus already claimed the ultimate victory.

The next day at the end of the school day Chelsea called and said she had to go back to the emergency room because she was feeling off again. I thought, "If I have to go back, I'm taking a friend with me," so I took my friend Nathan with me to meet Chelsea because if one can put a thousand to flight then two can put ten thousand to flight. Outside the emergency room, before I even stepped foot into the waiting room, I saw a woman and said "excuse me, I'm a pastor, can I pray for you?" What happened next was wild, as she began to scream, running into the emergency room and manifesting a demon saying, "Get away from me! Get away from me!" We followed her in, and as you can imagine, the whole place was looking at us (It wasn't necessarily the best entrance). I walked up to the front desk and said, "Hi, I'm Chris. I'm a pastor here to see my wife and my friend and I are going to ask people if we can pray for them." The person behind the desk must have been a Christian because he said, "sounds good!" We found Chelsea, who shared that she was wondering what was going on when the demonized woman ran into the waiting room but when she saw us she said in her head, "Oh the boys are here."

As we were waiting for Chelsea's name to be called, we began to pray for all the people around us. I turned to the person next to me and said "Hey you have pain in your neck, don't you?" The woman was shocked because she did. We prayed for her and nothing happened. Right after that, they called Chelsea's name, and as I was leaving Nathan stepped in and said, "Let me pray for you again." As I stood up to go back with my wife I turned to Nathan and loudly declared, "Hey you tell everybody out here, I will tell everybody in the backroom!" About 15 minutes later, I stepped out of the room and the woman that previously had the bad neck saw me and said "Hey what was that guy's name, and who is he?" (She was talking about Nathan). I told her that he was a pastor and she shared that the moment that he prayed for her the second time, she was totally healed. I could see she was in shock. I then began to tell the nurses and staff in the back about Jesus. It was amazing what happened that day, and my wife left the hospital completely fine.

I tell you this story because I wholeheartedly believe that we need to get our grit back as Christians. We need to remember how to fight again. If we get knocked down, that's fine but we cannot stay down talking about it for months, we need to learn to get up and simply hit back harder.

Our family did six months pioneering a Belong at Generation Church in St. Petersburg, Florida. While we were there, we faced a major attack. I'm not talking about little stuff that we often turn into big things, I'm talking about a major attack against my family. During that time, I'm happy to share that apart from one moment I can recall, we didn't miss any assignments that we were supposed to do when it came to travel, preaching, prayer, outreach, or discipleship. The one time I can recall us getting sidelined from our assignment was for one hour on an outreach day. I was out on outreach and got a call from Chelsea. She was in a hard place and was experiencing an anxiety attack that had become too much to handle with our four kids. The anxiety was due to a false accusation that was coming against our family. I quickly went home and Chelsea went into the room to pray. She came out one hour later and this is what she said, "Go back to work. We are not going to allow the enemy to stop us from doing what we are called to do." I went back out on outreach, went to Walmart, and three people were born again that day.

Why is this story so powerful? Because Chelsea could have said, "Let's just take a break for today and go back to work tomorrow." But she didn't. She said, "Go back to work." My wife is a gritty Christian. She understands that we don't fight against flesh and blood but principalities, powers, and rulers of darkness (Ephesians 6:12). We as the church need to become gritty once again. That is how we are going to take ground for the Kingdom.

DISCIPLESHIP IS NOT A PROGRAM, IT'S A FAMILY

Discipleship is not a program. Discipleship was never meant to be a program that we push people through. People know when they are just in a process and being moved onto the next step of the process. I'm not passionate about the Belong structure or the Belong program, I can take that or leave it. What I am passionate about is seeing people's lives transformed by the gospel and being added to my family. People desire to belong and be a part of something. People are hungry for family. This is a core conviction for us: That discipleship never becomes another meeting, class, or event.

We have people come to our Belong Gatherings all the time and say things like, "Wow this feels like family," or "Wow this feels like I found a home!" This is not because of the music or even the food or even the door greeter, it's because every person that is a part of our team understands that it is about the one and them truly becoming a part of the church family. This is why discipleship costs something. It will cost you your tight knit groups and cliques. It will cost you your time and personal space. One time Jesus was talking to a group of people and they said, "Hey your family is outside and they want to see you," and the bible says, "But he replied to the man who told him, 'Who is my mother, and who are my brothers?'" And stretching out his hand toward his disciples, he said, "Here are my mother and my brothers! For whoever does the will of my Father in heaven is my brother and sister and mother."

Do we actually treat people like they are family or do we just see them on the weekend in passing and use the word family? Some of my closest friends are those that I have won to the Lord and have discipled. Joel, James, Frank, Kyle, Rashad, Teddy, and more are names of guys that I had the opportunity to lead to Christ and have truly become a part of my family. It's very important to understand that discipleship was never meant to be Sunday school before worship, it was meant to be a life spent walking with people.

One of my favorite discipleship moments of the past few years was when we got to throw James Thomas a birthday party at Belong. James was the first person that ever came to Belong. My friend Adam led him to Jesus at an IHOP and then introduced him to me to disciple since he was not living in Fort Worth. James became family. My kids knew and loved him and would talk about him often. That Birthday party was so significant because we got to celebrate my brother James who never got to have birthday parties growing up, and I realized in a much bigger way that discipleship looks like family.

Make sure you never get so into a program that you forget to be family. I believe a mark of success is doing life with the people we lead to the Lord and having a whole lot of fun while we do.

PRAYER, OUTREACH, AND DISCIPLESHIP IS OUR FOCUS

It's important to keep the main thing the main thing. How do we keep the main thing the main thing? We don't just read books about it, talk about it, and have planning meetings about it: We do it. That's right, we do it. It's that simple. If you do what Jesus has called you to do, you will see results.

I know many pastors and leaders that don't share their faith outside of standing behind a pulpit on Sunday mornings. I know many churches that don't have prayer as a part of their weekly schedule. I know many churches that have no discipleship happening apart from Sunday mornings when they preach. These are not bad people or bad churches, they have just simply strayed from what we are called to do as the church.

So many churches get caught up in building the church that they don't have the time to go on outreach and disciple new believers. I'm all for great worship services, powerful messages, great production, kids ministries that are flourishing, and all the other things that go into a great Sunday morning experience, but I'm for prayer, outreach, and discipleship more. Why? Because I don't want to have a good church service that entertains Christians. I want to be part of a church that is preaching the gospel, casting out demons, healing the sick, and seeing people turn from the world to God.

I think it's possible to have both: A great Sunday service and a church focused on discipleship. I don't think that it needs to be one or the other. But if I have to choose, I'm choosing prayer, outreach, and discipleship over a perfect Sunday service every time.

While we were in Florida, I was given the opportunity to equip the church staff and take them on outreach one day. The production team, creative team, worship team, technology team, youth team, and admin team all showed up to be equipped and to go out and share their faith. For some it was their first time ever, for others it was only a handful of times in their life that they had shared the gospel outside of the church setting. After equipping them, we sent them out for a little over an hour. I went with Greg, the worship leader and Andrew, the video production guy. We had a wonderful time and were able to lead a man to the Lord in Walmart. That day when we all got back together to testify about what God had done, the team had many great encounters and ended up leading eight people to Christ! It was so powerful to see all of the different church teams come back excited to share what God had done. Greg the worship pastor later shared with me he was excited to have gone out because it awakened him, and he is now actively sharing his faith as he goes about his day. That's common because it's what we're created for. When we finally experience the glory of answering the call and seeing Jesus work through our obedience in everyday lives, there is nothing more fun or fulfilling.

When Jesus sent out the disciples, and later the 72, he didn't say "Okay, outreach team come over here, I'm sending you out to share your faith. Worship team, I'm going to send you out to practice worship. Creative team, can you go work on some creative t-shirt ideas to help us market my ministry? And oh, I almost forgot the hospitality team, can you get dinner ready?" That didn't happen. He said to all of them, "Go and preach the Gospel."

Somewhere along the way, we made outreach, prayer, and discipleship their own entities that some are called to. That's a lie. We are all called to share our faith. We are all called to pray. We are all called to make disciples. We as the church need to quit hiding behind excuses and simply respond to the call. We need to get out there and go for it.

If you are a pastor and you're reading this, it starts with you. If you don't do it, your people won't do it. Stop looking for the evangelist in your church or hoping one comes. Instead, start to do the work of the evangelist. If you don't have time in your schedule to share your faith, pray, and make disciples, I would like to kindly suggest you pause and fix your schedule. You should never be too busy to do what Jesus has called us to do.

The reason we successfully win people to the Lord is that we preach the gospel daily and we make room to disciple people weekly. If there is a secret it's that there isn't a secret at all. We do the work. We count the cost and we do what is necessary to answer the call. If you want to see it happen in your church and your ministry then share your faith, pray, and make space to disciple new believers.

GOD IS LOOKING FOR LABORERS NOT SUPERSTAR CHRISTIANS

Luke 10:2 states, "And he said to them, 'The harvest is plentiful, but the laborers are few. Therefore pray earnestly to the Lord of the harvest to send out laborers into his harvest.'"

The scripture doesn't state that the pastors, prophets, or evangelists are few. It doesn't state that the gifted are few, or even the well educated are few. It says that the laborers are few. I have taken this scripture to heart and I have responded to the call to labor with Jesus. It's important to understand that it is not glamorous when you enter into the labor of the Lord but it is glorious.

I grew up on a dairy farm in Woodland, Washington. I can remember the harvest seasons, whether it was hay, corn, or grass silage harvest. When it was harvest time, I knew what it meant: It was time to get to work. I knew that there would be long days and that I may be driving the truck until it was dark. When it wasn't harvest season, I knew when I was getting off work and could normally tell my buddies when I would be free to go ride dirt bikes or hang out. During harvest season, there was no saying how late we'd work. I didn't always enjoy it because it messed with my schedule. Sometimes I would try to rush and get done so I could get back to what I wanted to do. In doing so, I failed to understand that this harvest was one of the most important things for the farm to stay running and for the cows to be fed, which put food on our table.

One of the reasons I'm a successful evangelist is because I was taught the importance of good work ethic as a child and young adult. Today, I work for Jesus in the same way. When it's harvest time, I know what that means: It's time to get to work.

I have met many people who have disagreed with my thought process on working for the Lord. They would rather just fall in love with Jesus, and maybe the rest will happen by accident. The only problem with that approach is, people don't get saved. With that approach, Christianity has actually become all about self. With that approach, it would be easy to solely focus on ourselves and neglect the work that needs to be done.

I would say that one of the biggest things that have set me and our team apart thus far is that we work really hard for the Lord, whether we feel like it or not. We take honor in working in our Father's fields and in bringing in the harvest.

When I was 19 years old, I was newly saved and working on the dairy farm while attending Bible college. One of my jobs was to fix a fence on a piece of property that had cows on it. I was paired with an older farmhand that worked on the dairy farm longer than I had been alive. When we got to the fence, we began to tighten it. He was working on a specific section of the fence and when he was done he said, "That's good enough." The problem was when I looked at the fence, it was not tightened well. It still appeared loose and not properly fixed. I remember saying, "Hey man, that's not good enough. Let's do it right, let's make it great." He was older than me, he should have known better but he had become lazy in the field. I was young but I was the son of the farm owner. That fence was my dad's. Those cows were my dad's. I was not a hired hand, I was working as a son for my family business and I was going to put in the hard work to do it well.

Today, I think many in the church have become like the hired hand, they do just enough to get by yet, we're called to live like sons and daughters who work in our Father's field. We're called to work hard for the family business. It's time for the church to be sons and daughters who know what harvest time means: It's time to get to work. And when it's time to get to work, we need to be sons and daughters who do it with excellence because it's for our Father. It's for our family.

BAPTISM IN THE HOLY SPIRIT

We believe in the baptism in the Holy Spirit and are not quiet about it one bit. We believe the Bible and all that it has to say on this topic.

It's very easy to reason away this baptism if you have never experienced it before, which is sadly the case for many well-meaning pastors and leaders. People allow their experience or lack of experience to change what the Bible says about the Holy Spirit. The sad thing is, they do this thinking that they are helping the body of Christ avoid false teaching, while all the while they are keeping the body of Christ in a powerless state of Christianity. I believe many who do this end up becoming false teachers themselves because they preach against the Holy Spirit, even if they don't realize that they are doing so.

I believe in the Baptism of the Holy Spirit because I have experienced it, and because the Word of God clearly lays out that this baptism is for us today. Matthew 3:11 says, "I baptize you with water for repentance, but he who is coming after me is mightier than I, whose sandals I am not worthy to carry. He will baptize you with the Holy Spirit and fire."

Jesus is the one who baptizes with the Holy Spirit. I'm not going to lay out a complete theological argument in these sections about it but many amazing authors have written whole books on this topic that the church desperately needs to revisit again. What I do want to articulate is that baptism in the Holy Spirit and speaking in tongues is not something that we do on the side or behind closed doors because we are worried that we might upset somebody or freak someone out. That has been taught wrong. I believe the best way to honor people is to preach the pure Word of God. I want to honor God and preach his Word clearly and accurately so others, if they decide, can also be baptized in the Holy Spirit. Because we take this approach to the Baptism in the Holy Spirit, we experience people getting filled and speaking in tongues all the time. God spoke to me and said, "You preach it clearly and powerfully and I will come and baptize with the Holy Spirit."

This is what we see over and over again.

When I got saved, Casey, one of my closest friends, was a big part of my conversion and transformation. He would talk to me about the Holy Spirit and pray for me to receive it often. For three months, I asked and prayed to receive it but nothing seemed to happen. I hadn't had the big moment

I expected to have. I had this thought running through my head at that time, "I want a God encounter. I don't want to fake it until I make it." At that time in the church, some of the youth leaders with good hearts and excitement wanted me so badly to receive the Holy Spirit and speak in tongues that they were pressuring me. I didn't like that. If it was real, I wanted God to do it.

It's important to note that I grew up in religion that taught speaking in tongues was not for today. I can even remember hearing that speaking in tongues was of the devil. What's crazy to me is that somehow, amongst some, what God did to start the church in the book of Acts in the upper room has somehow been accredited to the devil. Excuse my attitude towards this religious mindset but that is a stupid, non-biblical conclusion to come to. I know that was strong but the truth is, it's a demonic lie to state speaking in tongues is of the devil.

After three months of seeking, praying, and asking God for this gift, my youth group headed to Seattle, Washington to go to a youth conference. It was my first Christian conference and TD Jakes from Dallas, Texas was one of the speakers. As he was preaching, he stopped and shared that the Holy Spirit was there in a specific way. I can remember the moment clearly because a moment later, out of nowhere, the Holy Spirit came in power and consumed me. I fell backward onto the ground and began to speak in tongues loudly. While I was on the ground God spoke to me and said "You are going to travel the world and preach the gospel. You are going to heal the sick, cast out demons, raise the dead, and cleanse the leaper."

At this time in my Christian walk, I had only been saved three months and didn't know that this was in the Bible. I didn't know that we could do these things if we believed and stayed in relationship with Jesus. After this experience, I can remember reading the book of Acts for the first time and thinking, "Oh wow! All that I heard him say to me is true. It's all in the Bible!" This experience with the Holy Spirit transformed and changed my life. From that moment forward there was a shift that put me on a course to do what I'm doing today. I can't imagine doing the Christian life without the baptism in the Holy Spirit.

The Holy Spirit is for all believers that ask for it. Acts 2:39 states, "For the promise is for you and for your children and for all who are far off, everyone whom the Lord our God calls to himself."

The promise of the Holy Spirit is for everyone whom the Lord calls, and he has called you.

SAVED, WATER BAPTIZED, BAPTIZED IN THE HOLY SPIRIT & DISCIPLED ASAP!

We have a strong New Testament conviction that when a person is saved they should be water baptized and baptized in the Holy Spirit shortly after salvation, along with being discipled immediately. In the western church, it's common for people to get saved and water baptized months later when the church does a formal baptism. Then, years later, they stumble across a YouTube video or book about the baptism in the Holy Spirit because the church didn't want to offend them with it when they first got saved. Up to this point, it's also common that they've only been discipled by the Sunday message weekly if they can even make it to church with their work schedule. Then, they are ultimately delivered the day that they die and go to heaven. This may sound dramatic but this is sadly true for many churches in America.

But why? Why can't people get saved, water baptized, filled with the Holy Spirit, and discipled all in the same week? The truth is they can, and I have seen it often. The reason it doesn't often happen in churches is because we have created systems and hoops to jump through. These systems and hoops are not evil but they slow down the process and ultimately they make it more about the process than the individual that was just saved and needs God. To be perfectly honest, I don't like church protocol if it's not set up for the individual that needs God to move in their life.

Another reason that we don't see this happen often is that people don't have time for it in their busy schedules. We have our church time on Sunday and the rest of the week is our time. When we live in this way we only have so much time on a Sunday to accomplish what needs to get done, so we begin to plan the year in quarterly baptisms. I'm all for planning but I fear if we are not careful we will plan the Holy Spirit and a true move of God right out of our services.

I want to be clear that I'm all for baby dedications, water baptism Sundays, Sundays that we invite the lost, youth Sundays, and different sermon series. I think all that is necessary and important. What I'm saying is that what God wants to accomplish simply cannot be accomplished on a Sunday morning. If we truly believe it's harvest time, we need to be ready to baptize people on the same day or within the same week that they receive Christ. We need to be ready to be inconvenienced and to make the main thing the main thing.

When Philip met the Ethiopian eunuch and preached the gospel to him this is what happened next, "And as they were going along the road they came to some water, and the eunuch said, "'See, here is water! What prevents me from being baptized?' And he commanded the chariot to stop, and they both went down into the water, Philip and the eunuch, and he baptized him." Acts 8:36, 38.

What I want you to notice is Philip didn't say, "Hey, we need to do this at church in a few weeks when Peter and your mom are there to watch." No, he baptized him because it was between him and God and he was ready to be baptized. I love structure, and as much as can be accomplished within it, but I want to specifically encourage you to never allow the structure to rob you from a spontaneous move of the Holy Spirit. Here is one of the many testimonies of everything I'm speaking of happening all in one day:

One Thursday Pastor Stephen, from Generation Church in Florida, and I went out on outreach together. It was a hot summer day in Florida and we were going door to door. I can remember saying to Stephen, "Let's call it and go to lunch," but Stephen said, "Let's go to one more house." We knocked on one more door.

Frank came to the door and we were able to encourage him and pray with him, as he was a believer who had lost his way and was hungry to come back into a relationship with Jesus. As we were leaving, a car pulled in the driveway of the house and it was a man named Kyle. We began to talk with Kyle and he told us that he was an atheist. We talked for a bit longer, shared the gospel with him, and prayed for him to encounter the presence of God. Pastor Stephen then asked if he wanted to give his life to Jesus, to which he said "Yes," and prayed to be born again right then and there. I remember him testifying about how he felt the peace of God come into his heart right after we prayed. We then invited both of them to Belong that night and they came. They both stood during the call for salvation and gave their lives to Jesus again (It's always a sign that God is really moving on a person's heart when they respond again). After the salvation call, we broke into groups to begin discipling the new believers that gathered and I can remember seeing them sitting with Pastor Stephen and in the Word of God and thinking, "This is what it's all about."

That night we had planned to do water baptisms in Pastor Stephen's pool and when Frank and Kyle heard that, they both shared they wanted to be baptized. Before we do baptisms we always take time to talk through the three baptisms: Salvation, water baptism, and Baptism in the Holy Spirit. I asked Frank and Kyle if they wanted to receive the baptism in the Holy Spirit and they both said yes. They were each baptized in water and when they came up out of the water, they were both filled with the Holy Spirit and began speaking in tongues.

I'm simply amazed as I think back on this story. A man who woke up as an atheist encountered Jesus, was saved, discipled, water baptized, and filled with the Holy Spirit all in the same day. Today, Kyle and Frank are both serving the Lord and growing in God because we created time to disciple and love them into the kingdom of God. And I think this is going to become the new normal. I think it needs to become the new normal. It's time to see people get all that God has for them so they can begin to truly thrive in Christ.

SABBATH REST & HAVING FUN

We believe in the sabbath. The sabbath is a day of the week that we don't work. The sabbath is more about what we don't do than what we do. We don't do anything that feels like work on the sabbath and we believe what the Bible says in Mark 2:27, "And he said to them, 'The Sabbath was made for man, not man for the Sabbath.'" It's very important that we rest and take a sabbath rest weekly. It's important to work hard and it's equally as important to rest well.

I will always let new believers know that I'm taking a sabbath on a certain day of the week and to not reach out to me because that time is set aside to rest and to be with my wife and kids. If we're going to stay rested and refreshed, it's vital that we honor and take a sabbath. Ministering to others becomes nearly impossible when we are depleted and tired. Resting is a non-negotiable if we're going to succeed in answering the call.

There are many great resources out there on the sabbath. My favorite is Robert Morris's book, "Take a break." I would encourage you to read it and to put its principles to work in your life. And I think it's important to say this before moving on to the next section: I have a life. I play basketball, I watch movies, I go shopping, I ride dirt bikes and street bikes, and I even watch the Portland Trailblazers and play NBA 2K with my grown-up friends. I prioritize rest and having fun all the time.

Why am I saying this? Because if you're not careful you will read my words and think, "Dang this guy has no life and is super serious." What I want you to understand is that you can enjoy life and fulfill The Great Commission at the same time, you just need to get really good at managing your time well.

Take a moment and take an inventory of your time. Remove the things that eat up your time, that you can live without and set aside time to rest and to have fun. Just decide you're going to be a full-time Christian all the time. If you remember, Jesus didn't stop being a Christian on the sabbath. He would do all kinds of things on the sabbath and the religious rulers would get angry. He would heal the sick and cast out demons while he was resting. How? Because it was the Holy Spirit doing the work through him.

One of the last outreaches I went on with our team in Florida, I decided instead of going on outreach that we would just go to the beach and play football instead. I needed a new football, so I stopped at Dick's Sporting Goods, shared the gospel while I shopped, and a lady was born again. We then grabbed some food before we hit the beach and as we did, a young man was born again. We then got to the beach and Josh and Aidan, two members of our team, were talking to Na'Im who was born again right before the football game began. Na'im came to church with us that Sunday and has been plugged into the local church ever since. How amazing! Just a group of people out to have a good time and rest, while sharing the gospel and enabling the Holy Spirit to move through them.

This is one of our core values within our ministry: If we're not having fun then we're doing something wrong. Don't be overly serious or get overly religious. Have fun and allow God to move through your life.

SECTION 2:
EVANGELISM PRAYER

We pray to move from our strength into God's strengths. It's so important to understand that we are not called to do the work of making disciples on our own or in our own strength. We are called to do the work in his strength and that cannot happen without powerful prayer times. Prayer is the engine to evangelism.

Let's look at the book of Acts for a biblical example of evangelism prayer:

"When they were released, they went to their friends and reported what the chief priests and the elders had said to them. And when they heard it, they lifted their voices together to God and said, "Sovereign Lord, who made the heaven and the earth and the sea and everything in them, who through the mouth of our father David, your servant, said by the Holy Spirit, "'Why did the Gentiles rage, and the peoples plot in vain? The kings of the earth set themselves, and the rulers were gathered together, against the Lord and against his

Anointed'— for truly in this city there were gathered together against your holy servant Jesus, whom you anointed, both Herod and Pontius Pilate, along with the Gentiles and the peoples of Israel, to do whatever your hand and your plan had predestined to take place. And now, Lord, look upon their threats and grant to your servants to continue to speak your word with all boldness, while you stretch out your hand to heal, and signs and wonders are performed through the name of your holy servant Jesus." And when they had prayed, the place in which they were gathered together was shaken, and they were all filled with the Holy Spirit and continued to speak the word of God with boldness."
Acts 4:23-31 ESV

They understood their need for God and that he is the one who works miracles, signs and wonders. We need to get back to prayer. Not prayer every once in a while but a life of continual, evangelism driven prayer. Our prayer time cannot stop at a good prayer meeting. Our prayer meetings need to lead to evangelism full of power and boldness.

I have met many people that tell me their call is prayer, and I don't disagree with that. I actually believe that we're all called to prayer. The issue is, I see many people say they're called to prayer, sitting with other believers praying, while holding the belief that others are called to do the work. I don't see that anywhere in scripture. I don't see Jesus saying, "Hey, prayer people, can you please stay back and pray so that the others will be successful in their outreach?" He didn't say that. He commanded all of us to pray and to go on outreach.

I believe people think this way for three reasons I want to share with you. I'm sure there are more reasons but here are three of my thoughts:

1. **People have not been taught the scripture accurately.** Many people are ignorant to the fact that all believers are called to make disciples. They go to a church that doesn't actively see the lost saved and discipled, and their leaders and pastors don't talk about it because they don't do it in their own personal lives. They are in a culture where this idea is completely foreign.

2. **People are scared.** Yes, I said it. People are scared to step out and share their faith with others. I believe that fear is one of the major reasons that people don't make disciples.

3. **People are lazy.** Quite simply, many people don't actually want to put in the work and effort that it takes to do the work of evangelism and discipleship. Remember, it's costly and it demands grit.

I know that was all pretty straight forward and those were perhaps difficult statements but I believe they're true. I believe those three reasons cause Christians to be inactive in sharing their faith and making disciples. The redemptive part is, prayer can and will shift all of that in a person's life. When someone prays and actively believes God for the lost to come into the Kingdom of God, they will begin to get his heart for people. When that happens, compassion will fill their heart and push them over the walls of fear and laziness. Remember, God is looking for people who are fearless and ready to labor in the harvest fields. It's important to remember that prayer will always fuel evangelism. Jesus spoke to the disciples and said, "Go and make disciples of all nations," but before he sent them to do it, he sent them to a 10 day prayer meeting to wait for the Holy Spirit to come upon them:

"And while staying with them he ordered them not to depart from Jerusalem, but to wait for the promise of the Father, which, he said, 'you heard from me; for John baptized with water, but you will be baptized with the Holy Spirit not many days from now.'" Acts 1:4-5 ESV

The disciples obeyed Jesus, prayed, and waited for the Holy Spirit to come. The Holy Spirit came and filled them and clothed them with power for the purpose of getting to work. The Holy Spirit didn't come so they could have a good Christian gathering. He came so that they could be clothed in power to take the gospel to people who desperately needed it. The same goes for us.

"When the day of Pentecost arrived, they were all together in one place. And suddenly there came from heaven a sound like a mighty rushing wind, and it filled the entire house where they were sitting. And divided tongues as of fire appeared to them and rested on each one of them. And they were all filled with the Holy Spirit and began to speak in other tongues as the Spirit gave them utterance." Acts 2:1-4 ESV

After they were filled with the Holy Spirit, they poured into the street with the power of God on them and 3,000 people were saved. If we truly want to see people saved and come into the Kingdom, then we need to be clothed with the power of God that can only happen in prayer.

Remember, the Holy Spirit is in you upon salvation, which is for you, and the Holy Spirit is on you upon being baptized in the Holy Spirit, which is for others. Without prayer you may be somewhat effective in going out but with consistent prayer and the baptism of the Holy Spirit you will be very effective.

Before I go further, I have a confession. I honestly can't believe I'm writing it in this book, especially in the prayer section of this book, but I hope that you can hear my heart as I share honestly with you: I often don't want to go to corporate prayer meetings because I think they are boring. Okay, I said it. I feel better getting that off my chest.

It's important you understand that in sharing that, I'm not talking about my relational prayer time I spend with Jesus in the mornings. It's very important that you understand I pray daily and connect with God on my own in my personal prayer life. I shared about this in the above section. I'm talking about corporate prayer times with others.

In my experience, so many prayer meetings are purposeless and powerless. They can become groups of Christians getting together and praying a wish list of prayers or praying prayers that are not relevant to what we are called to do here on earth. I have a hard time with people sitting and talking and praying but never actively winning anyone to Christ. I believe our prayer times should lead us to seeing the Kingdom of God expand here on the earth, and if they're not, something needs to shift or change. Some people may be satisfied sitting around and splitting hairs but I want to advance the Kingdom and break chains. I want to see people encounter the presence and the power of God. It cannot just be about a prayer gathering, as things will always get off if all we do is focus on one aspect of the call and the Kingdom of God. We are called to pray, to share our faith, and to make disciples. Prayer should always lead us to action.

In Matthew 9:37-38 it states, "Then he said to his disciples, 'The harvest is plentiful, but the laborers are few; therefore pray earnestly to the Lord of the harvest to send out laborers into his harvest.'"

I will never forget a conversation I had with a person at church who said, "I'm an intercessor and it's my job to pray to the Lord to send out laborers into the harvest field." I can remember thinking in my head, "The first person you are praying for is yourself."

I believe that we are all called to pray that prayer and we're all called to believe God will raise up an army to go out into the harvest fields. But I also believe that we are all called to respond to that prayer personally. Imagine this with me: A person in their prayer closet praying this specific prayer, "Lord send people out into the harvest fields and remove the mountains of fear that hold people back!" I can just see the Lord's response, "This sounds great. Let's start with you. The biggest mountain that needs to be moved is you not choosing to step out and share your faith with others." He would probably say it nicer...but I believe the Lord is saying to the Church "Move. I will be with you."

The Church has a tendency to fall into a trap of praying for revival and believing that it will just happen. I am no revival expert and I am definitely not claiming to understand the world of prayer and revival fully. I'm simply writing from my heart and experience and understand there are a lot of other good perspectives on this topic. I am not claiming to have this corner on the market at all. I just want to encourage you to ask yourself the question, "Is what I'm doing and believing bearing fruit?"

You see, my understanding is very simple. We must passionately pray for revival and then we must step out in faith and go for it. One of my spiritual fathers, Pastor Derril Corbin of Mannahouse in Portland, said to me once, "Momentum happens when God and man meet in the middle." Many people are praying that God will move, and God is saying back to us, "why don't you move and I will back you with power?"

"PRAYERS GO UP AND GOD IS LOOKING FOR PEOPLE TO CARRY THEM OUT"

Okay, what does this look like practically in a person's life?

I believe that prayers go up and then God is actively looking for somebody to carry them out. Let me explain what I'm talking about with a testimony:

A few years ago I was in the Philippines at the airport about to fly home. As we were walking into the terminal, I saw a man sitting right inside the door and I felt it impressed upon my heart to go over and talk to him. As we began to talk, he told me that he was from China and was about to fly home. I asked him if he was a believer and he said that he was not but that his wife in China was a very strong Christian. I knew at that moment that his wife had been praying for him and that God had sent me to share the gospel with him. After a good conversation, he prayed with me to be born again, accepted Jesus into his heart, and boarded his plane a saved man heading home to his praying wife.

I have so many stories like this, where I know God has led me to people that other Christians have been praying for. One time I was at a supermarket in Texas on outreach and I approached a couple that was shopping together. As I began to talk to them, I could tell that the wife knew the Lord and that the husband did not. As the conversation carried on, the wife said that she had been praying diligently for her husband to be saved. I explained the gospel to him right there and he decided to give his life to Jesus as his wife held his hands as he prayed.

Prayers go up and God is looking for people to carry them out. I have come to find that God has a prayer list for us. What I mean by that is this: People pray and God hears them. God has a list of prayers that need to be carried out and he's looking for people to help carry them out and see them answered. For me, I don't have a big prayer list. There are times that I make requests to God but they are pretty few and far between because I believe the Word of God where it states he already knows my needs. I do what Matthew 6:33 says, "But seek first the kingdom of God and his righteousness, and all these things will be added to you." I connect with God in the morning and when I walk out of my house I say, "Lord, I'm ready to partner with you, send me your prayer list." With that prayer and that heart posture, it amazes me how many divine encounters I have throughout the day as I just go about my life. And the best part is, just as the scripture says, if I take care of his Kingdom business then he takes care of all of my needs.

Sometimes for fun, I just like to imagine heaven when I wake up in the morning and walk out the front door. The angels must be like, "Guys, get ready! He prayed and connected with God and is looking to move in sync with heaven today. Set up the encounters, he is ready to be used!" I genuinely believe heaven gets excited when I go anywhere because the angels know that I'm not just going to pray, I'm going to actively step out and see the Kingdom of God come. I believe it's time for the church to pray powerful prayers and then step out in faith and partner boldly with all of heaven. I believe that if the church began to not just pray, but pray and step out in faith, more people would begin to show up to prayer meetings because prayer has always been meant to move us into activity in the Kingdom. Prayer is meant to activate us, that we may participate in what God is doing on the earth.

When the church begins to see prayers answered and the Kingdom of God moving around them, prayer will only increase and more people will begin to step out in faith. I have seen it often, and I have learned that the greatest way to get people involved in prayer and outreach is to simply do it. To allow the church to begin to see and hear the testimonies.

People get excited when God moves, people want to be a part of God moving because it's what we're created for.

While I was in Florida, a family who works at the church shared with me their children were greatly impacted by Belong and what we do. The reason for this is simple: They saw God move and it was exciting to them. They wanted to be a part of the action. We have too many prayer meetings and Bible studies that just scratch the surface of what we are called to as believers and Christians, that's hard to be excited about, but when God moves and people are healed, demons are cast out, people are water baptized and filled with the Holy Spirit speaking in tongues, there is a much greater buy-in because well, to be honest, it's real. It's not religious. And people want to be a part of something that is powerful and real.

HOW WE PRACTICALLY PRAY BEFORE WE GO ON OUTREACH

Before we go on outreach we take time to pray four specific prayers that we believe God has given us to pray. I'm sure there are many more amazing things that we could pray but we pray four specific prayers that we have seen yield great fruit time after time.

The four prayers are that we would:

1. **Be spirit-led**

2. Shift the atmosphere

3. Break chains off people's lives

4. And lastly, we pray, "Lord fill the nets because we believe that we cast the net but it is the Lord who fills the net."

Let me share a testimony with you that will show you the fruit of praying in this way.

Right after our team gathered and prayed these four specific prayers together and spent time worshiping and praying in the spirit, we headed out on outreach. I went to Tyrone mall in Tampa to start my day. Right as I walked through the door of the mall I got a word of knowledge for somebody's knees. I didn't know who it was for, so I put my attention on Jesus and asked him to lead me by his spirit. I then felt led to go into a barbershop near the entrance of the mall. As I walked into the barbershop, I was met by the owner who was a very cool guy. He actually cuts hair for the Tampa Bay Buccaneers football team! I asked him if somebody in the shop was having trouble with their knees. The shop was full, yet he quickly went over, turned the music off, and said "Hey, Los! This guy is asking if somebody has bad knees!" Los, a man in the barbershop, was blown away. He looked at me and said, "How did you know that about my knees?" At that moment, the entire barbershop was looking at me. The entire atmosphere of the barbershop had shifted and you could tangibly sense the presence of God.

I was able to explain to Los that God had spoken to me about him and that I would be happy to come back when he was done cutting the man's hair in order to pray for him to be healed. I came back about 30 minutes later and to my surprise, the entire barbershop that was just full was now empty and Los was sitting behind the front desk. I asked if we could pray for him and he said yes. As we prayed for him, a young man in our group laid his hands on him. After the prayer, Los looked over his shoulder at the young man and began to tell him that as he put his hands on him, he felt power go through his body and felt the pain leave. I then shared the gospel with him and he was born again right then and there, and the chains that moments prior held him bound were immediately broken off.

I was led by the spirit in the mall that day. Because God led me, the atmosphere shifted. Once the atmosphere shifted, chains broke. I went back and visited him multiple times while living there and it was always amazing to hear him share about what God was doing in his life.

Pray before you go, and then make sure you go.

FOUR SPECIFIC PRAYERS

1) SPIRIT-LED

There is a place that opens up in the spirit that is pretty amazing and hard to fully put into words, I want to do my best to try and describe it to you and my ultimate desire is that you would experience it for yourself.

There is normal evangelism and it is good and effective, it's a place that our teams operate out of often. I call it normal because when we are out on outreach, it feels pretty normal. You know that God is with you and things are happening in the spirit around you and lives are being impacted, but it feels like what we call a workday. Some days outreach is just plain, hard work and we embrace those days, plow the ground, and plant the seeds in people's hearts because we know what we are called to do. We grind it out in obedience to the call.

Then, there is what we call "Spirit-led supernatural evangelism," which is like jumping into a massive river that just carries you to where you need to be, to who you need to talk to, and into situations that have undeniably been made ready for Jesus! Spirit-Led evangelism is powered by prayer and hearts seeking to be in tune with the spirit. Before I continue, I want to make sure that you understand that I'm not spiritually weird, or at least I don't think I am. I have experienced people on outreach attempting to follow the spirit so hard that it can actually feel exhausting to be around. They pray about every aspect of the outreach and press into God about where they should go to lunch, McDonald's or Burger King, and to be honest I'm like, "Neither let's go to chick-fil-a, that's the Lord's chicken!"

There is a moment however, when you know you have tapped into spirit-led evangelism, and it becomes undeniable. It doesn't feel like work, it feels like being swept up in a wave of the Holy Spirit. In those moments, it begins to seem effortless. Things begin to happen around you in a manner that you cannot fully explain with your natural mind.

While we were in Florida it took a few months until we broke through and broke into this but when we did, we found ourselves saying over and over again, "Wow! Only God could do that!"

I've come to find that to break into this spirit-led evangelism, one must pray and ask God to lead them by his Spirit. Wherever you live, there are people all over the city ready to encounter God and ready to say "Yes" to Jesus. You just need to find them and there is no better way to find them than to allow the Holy Spirit to lead you straight to them. I want to be clear that every time I go out, I don't enter right into spirit-led outreach and start flowing in that supernatural river. Sometimes we have a day of working and plowing like I was writing about earlier. That could look like knocking on doors for hours trying to find the people that are ready, getting rejected 20 times over, and finding one person or home that is ready for the gospel. This kind of evangelism works and has its place, just going out and working the fields until you find the people that are open to receiving the gospel, but when you get in that river, it carries you right to the people. And it feels so easy it almost feels as if it were an accident. I use the phrase accident because in these moments of Spirit-led outreach things happen without any effort or thought. It's difficult to explain but things just begin to happen.

Let me tell you some testimonies to help explain what I'm talking about:

One day before we went out we prayed this prayer, "God lead us by your Spirit." After praying, one of our team members felt led to go to a specific street. We went to that street and began to go door to door. A few houses in, we walked up to a home that a young man was sitting outside of on the porch. That young man looked at me and said, "Hey, I know you, you talked to me at Sam's Club a few months ago." When I looked at him I realized it was true. A few months prior, I was on outreach and stopped and talked to him in the parking lot. He was the cart guy. I shared the gospel with him that day but at that time he was not ready to say yes to Jesus. By God's spirit, in a county of 1 million people, we were led right to his door months later. After talking with him, he prayed to give his life to Jesus.

Another example of this happened just recently. My family and I just moved back to Woodland, Washington for six months to establish Belong for The Promise Church. Three years ago when I lived there, I had the privilege to lead a practicing Wiccan named Kimberly to the Lord. She got saved, started to come to church, was water baptized, and filled with the Holy Spirit. The church helped her get her tiny home finished and came around her to really help and support her. At that time, her husband was in jail so I didn't have the opportunity to meet him or lead him to Christ (He claimed to be a Christian but really needed to be born again). Three years later, our family was driving back from Portland and decided to stop in Vancouver, Washington to eat some Panda Express (My kids love the orange chicken… okay so do I…). As I was sitting at the table, I began to talk to a man that was near me waiting for a take-away order. As the conversation continued, he realized that I was the guy that led his wife to the Lord three years prior when he was in jail.

At that moment, he ran out of the restaurant to get Kimberly and to tell her that I was back in town. They were so blown away, and to be honest, so was I. When you get into that place in the spirit and things begin to happen, it will truly blow your natural mind away. You will experience things only God could set up for you.

At that moment, I was able to share with him about Jesus and at the time of writing this, I am planning to meet them for dinner so that he can hear the gospel and hopefully be born again. What's incredible is that in a massive city, I ran into Kimberly's husband three years later. And to be honest, these kinds of things happen to me all the time and I desire to live in this place all the time. Some days are more difficult than others, we plow and we do the work, but I always look forward to the days when we get to live in God's divine river that makes evangelism supernaturally easy. When we take the time to pray and allow God to lead us, he leads us in a way only He can. He leads us to people who are ready for the gospel, and sometimes He even leads us to complete the work He began in a family through our obedience three years prior. Only God can do that.

I want to encourage you to pray daily on an individual level to be led by the spirit and to pray corporately before you go on outreach. Pray to be led by the spirit and to be led to the people who are ready to receive Christ.

I was recently in Bend, Oregon on a personal prayer retreat and decided to go door to door one afternoon. I have grown in confidence knowing that the spirit will lead me as I go.

Pastor Phil and two others came along with me to share the gospel. As we drove, I prayed to the Lord that he would lead us by His spirit. I could feel the spirit as we got out of the car and just knew something was going to happen.

At the fifth house, a man named Mark came to the door. I asked if I could share the gospel with him and he said "Yes." He welcomed me into his home and as I began to share with him I asked him if he was born again and he said, "No, but I'm really close." I knew at that moment and even said to him, "God led me to your door. I'm not from your city. I'm here on a prayer retreat but God led me to your door to lead you to Christ." We read John 3 together and he prayed to give his life to Jesus. He had tears in his eyes as he prayed to be born again and at the reality that Jesus had sent someone to His door.

We need to be led by the Holy Spirit and that can only happen when we pray, step out in faith, and go for it.

I want to say one more time that some days feel normal, and normal often feels like just plain, hard work in the harvest fields. I want to be honest with you so that you're set up for success. There may be people out there that say that it should never be that way, that you should always be flowing in the spirit and it should be easy. While I wish that were true, my experience as a farmer and a son tells me otherwise.

I believe that it often starts in one region with prayer and hard work. From there, things begin to open up and the supernatural river begins to flow. In Florida, that took about two months of putting our heads down to pray and then putting our hands to the plow to work the fields. In doing so, we broke through, chains broke, and lives were transformed. So begin to believe God will lead you by his spirit, and pray and put your hand to the plow as you prepare!

2) ATMOSPHERE SHIFTING

We are called to be thermostats, not thermometers to the world around us. We are called to shift atmospheres wherever we go and to bring the Kingdom of God to earth. We cannot shift the atmosphere by ourselves with our awesome energy or great personality, we need to carry the authority of heaven within and upon us so that we can truly see things shift and change around us.

There is a scripture that I love in Matthew 28:18, "And Jesus came and said to them, 'All authority in heaven and on earth has been given to me.'"

Jesus clearly states that all authority in heaven and on earth has been given to him. It doesn't say that it's been given to us. It's been given to him. Why is it important that we understand this simple but true fact? Because if we don't have Him, we don't have real authority. If we don't have real authority, we do not have what it takes to transform and change the people and atmospheres that we are in and around.

There are people that run around thinking they have authority in themselves because of a special title, or because of Christian fame they have acquired, or because they are gifted and can move a church congregation to tears. Gifting is wonderful but gifting and the authority that comes from truly knowing Jesus are entirely different things. We shouldn't need the atmosphere to shift in a church meeting. If it's a church that is built on the truth and worships in spirit and in truth, it should already be shifted and full of the presence of God. I need the atmosphere to shift at Walmart when I'm shopping. I need the atmosphere to shift on an airplane when I'm traveling. I need the atmosphere to shift in the coffee shop when I'm with my kids. Wherever there are people that need to encounter Jesus and need to be saved, I need the atmosphere to shift.

We need Jesus and his presence in order to have real authority to shift atmospheres. This is why we take time to pray, that wherever we go we will shift the atmosphere and see heaven come to earth. We take time to pray and connect with God before we go out so that we have Christ's power upon us so that we can see things change in a powerful way.

Have you ever walked into a restaurant or a clothing store or a place of business and felt darkness? I often do, but I also understand I'm not supposed to leave that place in the same state it was in when I walked into it because Christ in me is greater than what's in the world.

Remember, that authority is about who you know, not what you think you know. If we don't take time to connect with God and seek him and his presence daily, we will lack anointing and will live as powerless Christians who do not see atmospheres shift around us. If we pray to be clothed in power and to walk hand and hand with Jesus, we will begin to see God move through us in power everywhere that we step. Here is a testimony that will help me explain the authority that shifts the atmosphere:

In 2018, my friend Aaron and I had the amazing opportunity to go to Iraq to visit a missionary and his family that had been doing wonderful work for the Lord for years. As we were there, a supernatural door opened for us to go into a mosque to give away food and to share the gospel. In this situation, we prayed and asked God to shift the atmosphere in that place when we went in so that the people there would encounter the presence of God in a real, tangible way.

Right before we got there, I received a word of knowledge in the van for healing. Oftentimes, God will speak to me for others so that they will know that God is real and that he loves them. My friend decided that after the welcome, we would pray for the sick and share the word of knowledge that I had received about healing. When we were in the mosque, I shared the word of knowledge that I had received from God. There were over 300 people and a woman in the third row of chairs on the right hand side stood up and shared that the word was for her and that she wanted prayer. As we began to pray, without anybody touching her, she fell over onto the ground under the power of God. When she stood up, she was completely healed, and while that occurred many more in the room experienced healing in Jesus name.

The atmosphere was completely shifted and the gospel was preached clearly immediately after that. The presence of

God came and many, if not all, in the mosque raised their hands to receive Jesus as Lord that day.

It was difficult to follow up, so we don't fully know what happened with all those who prayed, but we do know the seed of the gospel went into their hearts. That day I got to witness the atmosphere shift in a very dark place in one, single moment. Why did it happen that way? Because we prayed and asked God to shift the atmosphere. And despite pressure that came the night before saying we couldn't preach the full gospel in a mosque, my friend David preached the full, true gospel that day.

Jesus backs his Gospel. Jesus backs a praying people who step out in faith to advance the Kingdom of God. I want to encourage you to begin to pray that the places that you go begin to shift entirely and that God would open up opportunities for you to share the true gospel. As this happens, I think you're going to come alive by what you experience and see. There is no greater way to live!

3) CHAIN BREAKING

We sing songs about breaking chains and preach messages about chains breaking off our lives and the lives of those around us. We are called to live free in Christ and to help the world understand that they can live free as well. This should be our reality and the invitation we're extending to the world as believers because many are in chains.

Let me define what I see as a chain in a person's life: It is something that holds them down and keeps them chained to the world and its system. Chains hold people bound to something and they limit their ability to be free in Christ or to know Christ at all.

I believe that when we are led by the spirit and the atmosphere shifts because the presence of God comes in power, chains fall off of people's lives as a byproduct. Think about the story in the section above about the mosque. A supernatural door opening because of the leading of the Holy Spirit and then the atmosphere shifting because of prayer and obedience to preach the gospel. Chains of the Muslim religion and sickness began to fall off of people's lives. When I think about a chain, I'm not thinking about a small chain necklace, I'm thinking about a massive chain that cannot be removed with human strength alone. There are people that are bound in massive chains that cannot get free with all of their own human effort, study, self-improvement plans, diets, medications, and even religious routines. People need to have an encounter with God to be set free from the chains that hold them down. Chains of depression, suicidal thoughts, homosexuality, fear, anxiety, control, manipulation, and many more things that I don't have room to list. These chains have to be broken by the presence of God. Only Jesus can truly set people free from the chains of the world.

We pray that we can be used by God to be chain breakers in the Kingdom of God because we want to see people get saved and walk in freedom for the rest of their lives. Here is a testimony that will help me communicate what I'm trying to say:

I had the honor to walk with somebody as they walked out of a lifestyle of homosexuality. This person claimed to be a Christian, and in their mind, had found a way for the Bible to support their belief system. We planned to get coffee and to talk about the issue and they told me after the conversation that they had planned to come to our lunch meeting to let me have it and to tell me that I was wrong and that they were right.

When we sat down, something totally different happened because they sat down and were met with the presence of God. In the presence, something called Godly conviction began to grab hold of my friend. They said to me, "Man I can feel the presence of God, and I'm so convicted that I'm wrong and you are right." This meeting that we had was the start of a transformation that was so powerful to witness. God did a mighty work in a heart that so desperately needed him. And what I want to specifically highlight from this story is this: God did a work. I didn't set them free. I couldn't. God was the one who set them free. Why is that important to understand? Because we can't break chains off of people's lives that hold them bound in sin and darkness. What we can do is be a carrier of the presence of God and hold a Biblical standard that breaks chains off people's lives so they can walk in freedom.

Back in the day when I was newly saved and had a new passion for telling people about Jesus, myself and a group from church began to go to downtown Portland to share our faith and feed the homeless that were there in the downtown parks on Friday nights. So many amazing things happened during those times. That's where I really began to see God move in power. One Friday night, we began to minister at a bus stop. There was a girl waiting to catch a bus, so the girls in the group were ministering to her and then began to pray for her. I was about 10 feet away watching and all of a sudden the girl's face changed right in front of my eyes. I watched as her face morphed into the face of a demon and the demon began to laugh at me and the group. The girl's voice changed and was clearly manifesting a demon. This was the first time that I had ever witnessed something like this. I didn't have a manual with me or any experience, so I walked over to her and actually put my hand around her neck, and began to pray in the spirit. I would not have done it that way today. I would have put my hand on her shoulder. As I began to pray, I watched as the devil left her in a moment. The chains broke off of her the moment I began to pray. All of a sudden she said, "I need to go home and see my mom. I have been away from home living the wrong way. I need to change!" She then got on the bus and drove away. At that moment, the chains that were previously on her life and the assignment of that demon were all broken off completely. God led us to that bus stop by his Holy Spirit, the atmosphere shifted as the girls began to pray in the name of Jesus, and the chains that bound her were broken off completely. Spirit-led, atmosphere shifting chain-breaking. That is what the Lord does with our prayers and our obedience.

I want to encourage you to begin to pray that wherever you go you begin to see chains fall off of people that need freedom in their lives. I believe we are called by God to be chain breakers for the world around us.

4) FILL THE NET

"God fill the net! We are here today telling you that we are ready to answer the call to disciple the nations. We are praying and asking for you to fill the net. We have created time and space for people and we are ready to disciple them. We just need you to send them to us."

This is a prayer that we pray every time that we are in the prayer room before we head out on outreach. God spoke to me and said, "If you create a net, I will fill it." That simple statement that he said to me one night in a vision changed the way that I operate and think about prayer, outreach, and discipleship.

God wants to fill your net with people that are ready to be discipled and are hungry for God. It's important to understand that you first need to have a net for him to fill. I know that this is a very simple concept but he can't fill a net you don't have. Remember, a net is just simply time and space to disciple people. There is no point in praying to God to fill the net if you don't have one.

The first step is to create time and space for the specific purpose of discipling people. Once that net is created, you can pray bold prayers and ask God to fill your net with people. When you've done the work to create the net, you can pray with such confidence and expectation. This is always the last prayer that we pray before we go out on outreach because it reminds us that God is the one who ultimately fills the nets with people.

I believe that if pastors and leaders would begin to do this in their churches, God would begin to send the people to fill the empty rows that other marketing strategies and creative sermon series haven't seemed to be able to fill. I believe that it's time to get back to the roots of making time and space for what really matters. A new church sign, logo, website, or marketing campaign is great but creating space to do what God has called us to do is better. And it will bring about great fruit.

God knows that I have created space for discipleship and I pray and seek God daily to send me people that I can walk with. I've done my part, and what he does is he sends them to me. Sometimes in the most amazing ways. I'm going to share two testimonies with you that are so incredible because you will see God in the details. These stories will help you further understand the concept of creating space for people and God sending the people:

I travel quite often to speak at churches and conferences. One day, I was at the Portland, Oregon airport about to fly back home to Dallas, Texas. I was running a bit late for my flight so I was in a hurry and was power walking to my gate once I made it through security. As I was walking, a guy was walking beside me at about the same pace. I always share with the people that are walking beside me heading in the same direction. He was wearing a Portland Trailblazer hat so

I started talking to him about the NBA and the Blazers, which is my favorite team. As we were talking, I knew that I would shift the conversation to Jesus. When I changed the topic to Jesus he was very interested and excited, he began to tell me that he was coming back into a relationship with Jesus. We exchanged numbers and stayed in contact for the next few months. He lived in Portland, Oregon and I lived in Fort Worth, Texas. At that time, he didn't know it but his company was about to offer him a job that would move his family to the Fort Worth, Texas area. Six months after meeting him in an airport, he was sitting in my living room in Texas at Belong, being discipled with his wife and daughter.

Through this story and so many others, I began to see that God is so interested in people being discipled that he will work the details out in crazy, supernatural ways just to set up discipleship for his kids.

I believe that somebody else could have discipled him and his family but other people probably didn't make the time and space for discipleship. Other people probably didn't ask the Lord to fill the net they had created. In obedience, I did. In God's faithfulness, he filled it and continues to. I will never forget the night that he was water baptized in my backyard and came out of the water speaking in tongues. It's a story only God could write. I was just hurrying to my gate but I had done the work to be ready. I had a net and I asked God to fill it.

Another story I love was when I was at the Tampa Bay, Florida airport getting picked up for a weekend with

Generation Church. At that time, I lived in Fort Worth, Texas, and was planning to move to Florida for a six-month season six months from that time. I was sitting in the vehicle that came to pick me up waiting for my two friends that flew in on a different flight to make it to the car so we could head to dinner. As I was waiting, I thought to myself, "Why not share with somebody about Jesus?" I rolled my window down in the car and said to a woman that was standing there, "Hey, I just want you to know that Jesus loves you." I say that same thing very often and get many different responses from people. The response that I got this time was not expected. The woman began to walk toward the car and said to me, "Do you know why I'm here?" I was thinking that somebody died or that she was getting cancer treatment the way that she said It. I said, "please tell me why." She excitedly shared that her son was just born again two days ago. I instantly knew that God was up to something. I stepped out of the car to talk to her, and as I did, her son Cody came walking up. We began to talk and he told me that he was at a store and an older woman approached him and shared the gospel with him and he was saved. I was able to pray for him and get his number because he needed discipleship and a church home. He lived about 45 minutes away from where I was going to be but said that he would be at church that Sunday. He came to church that Sunday with his mother. I told him that I would be coming back in six months and would love to have him come to Belong and be discipled. The church was also doing baptisms two weeks from that Sunday and he wanted to be water baptized, so I flew back in to see him and water baptize him two weeks later. It was powerful. When I arrived in Florida six months later, Cody faithfully came to Belong. The first Belong we ever had in Florida he was the only person that came, and I love that because all that we do is about the one. We were so excited about him being there, we gave him the VIP experience. That first night he shared his testimony with us and we all cried listening to what fully happened that day that he was saved. We then prayed for him to be filled with the Holy Spirit and to speak in tongues, and he did right there on the living room floor.

I had created a net for discipleship that was six months out and God went six months before me to fill it. This is how much God cares about his kids. This is how much God cares about discipleship. The Lord knew that Cody needed to be discipled, water baptized, and filled with the Holy Spirit. The Lord knew that we would make time to do it, so he set up a divine encounter at the airport while I was waiting for my friends to make it happen. I want to encourage you: Create a net and pray that God will fill it because he will!

A few years ago I was in Seattle, Washington speaking at a small church gathering in a leader's home. Leaders were invited to gather and I shared a message centered around evangelism. After the message, I got into a conversation with a youth pastor from the area. This youth pastor loved the Lord and was truly a great guy. As we were talking, he was telling me about his passion for discipleship and shared that it's what God called him to do. I asked him who he was discipling and he shared that he was focusing on four boys who were in his youth group. His youth group consisted of a few youth from families who attended the church. He then began to tell me that there was a big high school across the street from the church that had over a thousand students in it, but that he felt like the Lord said to focus on these four in the youth group, not the school full of students that needed to encounter God. As I listened to him, I began to get concerned. Again, he was not a bad guy. He loved the Lord and wanted to fulfill The Great Commission to disciple people. The more he talked, the more I could so clearly see what I had seen in many other conversations with loving pastors and leaders: They put outreach and discipleship into two different categories. From there, they convince themselves they are called to the discipleship category, not the outreach category. Many people in the church today share that mindset and it is stopping the Kingdom from expanding and people from being saved.

I don't believe that you can have ongoing discipleship without ongoing outreach. I believe people have redefined discipleship and removed the new believer portion of it so that they can feel better about their Bible studies filled with Christians. I believe that all believers need discipleship and need to grow in the Lord but let's not forget what Jesus said, "Go and make disciples," which means that we are actively winning people to the Lord and discipling them. The youth pastor I spoke to was in an amazing location to be a light to a school and students in need. I don't believe he was hearing God in his decision to focus only on the youth group that he had at the time. He shared with me that he didn't think he could disciple all the students that may come from the High School, so because he didn't think that he could disciple them, he didn't want to share Jesus with them. I began to share with him that he needed to think bigger, that he needed to believe God for his supernatural help, and that he would send a team to help him disciple the kids that would begin to come to the Lord. As the pastor, he felt the responsibility to disciple every person personally, which would be simply impossible. We need to have a team of people that are equipped to help us disciple those who are saved. I have a strong conviction that every believer should be discipling a new believer. One of the issues that we have in the church is that we hire staff and pay them to disciple people, which is great but where it begins to hurt us as the church is we hire them and somehow think that gets us off the hook to disciple people as well. If we call ourselves a Christian, we're called to disciple.

A few years ago I began to ask myself if I was crazy because if you don't know me, I share my faith everywhere, all the time. I don't need to be on an outreach to share my faith. I simply believe we are called to live as full-time Christians, which looks like sharing Jesus at gas pumps, grocery stores, parks, and anywhere that our feet take us throughout the day. I believe that outreach is biblical, Jesus sent them out two by two. I believe that mission trips are important, however, I believe that if every Christian would live on mission every day, wherever their feet walk, we would see many people come to know Jesus. Early on in my walk with Jesus, I was around people that would challenge me on my walk and the way that I shared my faith so often. They would say things like, "you're a bit over the top" and "if you're not careful you're going to burn out." The people that have said things like this to me in the past said it in love, thinking that they were helping me to avoid burnout or a legalistic work-based approach to God.

I can remember hearing their heart as they spoke but I fear they had already allowed their flame for evangelism to burnout. I wrestled with this for years thinking, "Man, am I crazy? Am I too intense? Do I need to stop telling everybody that I come into contact with that Jesus loves them? Do I need to stop trying to share the gospel with them? Do I just need to slow down and take the easy road? Maybe the people that talked to me are right. I can just be a little bit calmer and still do amazing things for Jesus..." Then I heard the Holy Spirit one day very clearly. He said to me, "What do you think a person full of the Holy Spirit and power of God that has no fear would look like?" My response was, "Well, the Holy Spirit talks about Jesus, so that person full of the Holy Spirit would be talking about one thing to people who were lost and that's Jesus!" From that day on, I have never entertained the thought that I'm too over the top or too concerned about telling others about Jesus. And the truth is, the way I live convicted the people who sought to change me, suggesting I look more like a lukewarm church. I won't do it, and I know I'm not crazy. I'm just a full-time Christian who has put their hand to the plow and never looked back.

One thing I often hear now from people is not, "Slow down," or "Be careful." Today I hear, "Wow, it's awesome that you are doing this work for the Lord. You're an evangelist, that is what you're called to do!" I do understand that I am an evangelist. I understand that I'm going to be a bit more focused and will most likely talk to more people than the average believer but as an evangelist, it's my job to equip the church to do the work of evangelism. As an evangelist, I will do things that other believers won't do, like speak in front of big crowds at a church or a crusade field in another country, or go on mission trips to dangerous countries to preach the gospel. I want you to understand that I believe those are things that I'm called to that may differ from other believers. Those things mentioned are different from sharing your faith one on one with the people that you are around daily and I understand that but we are all called to share our faith.

One time I made a post on social media about all believers sharing their faith daily and a pastor from a nearby city responded and shared that they were happy they were the other five-fold ministries that focus on topics apart from evangelism. They then asked me in the comment section what my definition of an evangelist was, my response was, "An evangelist is called by God to equip the Body of Christ to do the work of evangelism starting with the pastor, teacher, prophet, and apostle." To be honest, some church leaders don't want that to be true because then they will be responsible to share their faith and win people to the Lord. I believe in the balance of the five-fold ministry, the issue that I see is, like this pastor, people want to focus on what they are comfortable with.

Jesus had the five-fold ministry within him; he was the greatest pastor, teacher, evangelist, prophet, and apostle to walk the earth. When Jesus spoke out The Great Commission he didn't say, "This is just for the evangelist to do. Everybody else gets to hang back and be comfortable in their air-conditioned church services." No, because The Great Commission was to go. It was an apostolic call. The mission and the aim are to preach the gospel and make disciples. Somewhere along the way we have gotten off course and have made it about conferences, small groups, and prophetic nights. Listen, I'm good with all of that stuff if it is fulfilling the call of making disciples.

I know I sound like a broken record saying the same thing over and over again but as I sit here writing this, my heart is burning for people to understand that it is really simple. We just have to begin to focus on the right things. We just have to begin to pray, go on outreach, and disciple people. I can hear the voices of the pastors, teachers, and prophets saying we need to balance all of this but if I'm honest, I'm really over all of the religious games. I can hear the voice of God louder saying, "Go and make disciples."

I want you to understand how seriously I take evangelism. It's not something that I do sometimes, it's a way of life and I take personal responsibility for my city. I want to see the church begin to take responsibility for their cities. Below is a testimony to help you see how much energy we put towards going after the lost in our city. I hope that this testimony encourages you and others to step out in faith and believe God for people to be saved because until believers have a burden for their cities to know Christ, they will remain fruitless in reaching the lost within it. You need to ask God to share his heart with you for your city so that compassion can move you to action. God shares his heart with his friends in the secret place, so get in your secret place and ask God for his heart.

I grew up and lived in the small town of Woodland, Washington for 31 years. It's an amazing city that has grown over the years. Many of the fields in town that were once farmland are now filling up with houses. I got saved at age 18 and became activated in evangelism around age 19 when a Bethel Church team came to our church and took us on outreach. From that moment, I really began to daily share with people about Jesus.

A few years into the journey of stepping out and growing in God I began to say, "When everybody from my town stands before God, I want them to be able to say Chris Donald or somebody from The Promise Church told me." Told them what? That Jesus can save them from their sins and give them eternal life. I had decided I wanted to make it really hard for anybody in my town to go to hell. One day, while I was praying, God gave me an idea of doing a tent meeting in Woodland City Park. At that time, I was one of the senior leaders at the Promise Church, so I presented the idea to the team and they said let's go for it. We had a few weeks to pull it off.

We called the event "Hope in the Park." The plan was to do a two-day event at the park with giveaways, free food, worship, and a gospel message. What was even better was that we were going to do a full-on strategic campaign that had three components to get the word out about the event. A paid social media ad for our region, an army of church members to go door-to-door the week before, and a group of us to stand on the side of the freeway with signs. We did it and it was amazing. The day we went door-to-door, Chelsea and I went to a house and a lady answered the door. We handed her one of our "Hope in the Park" flyers that we were giving out to people. She said, "Hey, I have seen this on Facebook and I saw this same thing the other day on the side of the road on the Woodland off-ramp! People were holding this sign up." I then got a word of knowledge that somebody in their family was dealing with stomach issues, so I asked her and shared what I felt God shared with me. At that moment, she was blown away because her husband was upstairs struggling with Crohn's disease. I asked if I could pray for him, but unfortunately he was not available at that time. Thankfully she said that they would come to "Hope in the Park." She ended up coming and I was able to meet and pray for her husband and connect with the family. It was amazing, and it wouldn't have been possible unless we decided to step out and do something.

Hope In The Park was on a Friday and Saturday and that Sunday, directly following, our church attendance was up by 50 people. For our church, that was amazing. We had 50 new people in the church that Sunday who heard the gospel preached and experienced the presence of God. It was really amazing fruit because we took Jesus at his word and stepped out in faith.

What could happen if you stepped out in faith? I can remember standing on the side of the road for two days holding a sign that said "Jesus loves you" leading up to the event. The city of Woodland has two off-ramps and most people take the first one that enters into the main part of the city at exit 21. As I stood there, we got all kinds of feedback. Some people flipped us off and others said "Amen," but most of all what I was doing, no matter the response, was trying my best to make the name of Jesus known in my city.

If you're reading this, I want to encourage you to get out of the box, get into your community, and engage the lost. If you are not seeing new people come to your church or youth group, it's time to change what you're doing because it's not working. Maybe you need to take a day of your week to go on outreach for a few hours. I know that you probably don't want to because, well, if you did want to you would probably be doing it already, but I want to do my best to encourage you whether you want to or not.

While I was on staff at The Promise church, I would lead summer park outreaches. These outreaches were so much fun. We would go to Cash and Carry and buy 300 dollars worth of hot dogs, chips, and drinks and head to the park with a pop-up tent and some cool church signs. We would start up the bbq, set up a volleyball net, and begin to talk to people about Jesus. Once the hot dogs were done we would load them up and walk around the park to hand them out and pray for people. We saw so much fruit from these outreaches and they were so much fun. I believe that if you say yes to engaging your community, God will give you creative ideas to make Jesus known.

We are now going to shift gears and get to the more practical equipping part of the outreach section. Below are three different sections that cover our heart, our approach, and follow-up strategies to be effective on outreach and with discipleship. These are a great resource for you and if you are leading a team, you will be able to use these to help equip them as well.

OUTREACH | OUR HEART

Be Led By love!
For Jesus, Compassion Was The Motivation
For His Miracles

Compassion needs to be the motivation for your outreach. People know and can feel love. They can also sense when people are trying to pressure them to do something. Jesus was moved by compassion; this is why he had such an open door with sinners because they knew that his motives were pure. He wasn't trying to sell them anything, he wasn't trying to trick them, he was simply loving them with the love of God in his heart.

Boldness Without Compassion Is Dangerous

I have been on many outreaches with many different people and have experienced people that, if I'm honest, were too bold and forgot that it was about the people they were trying to reach, not about them doing something crazy for God. Oftentimes, the people who do what appears to be the boldest things are actually the most scared. I know that's a little bit confusing but give me time to explain.

There was a guy that I met who would travel from city to city, walk into restaurants and places of business, and loudly declare, "I'm here to tell you that you need to be saved. If you want to hear more, meet me outside and I will talk to you." Then, he would walk out and wait. Sure, maybe a person every once in a while would walk out and talk to him but if

I'm honest, that is just weird. To a person that has no grid for the gospel or evangelism, they would probably be thinking, "That guy is crazy!"

This guy came to a church meeting that I was at with a well-known speaker and he stood up, in the middle of the meeting, and told the speaker to repent as he was walking out of the meeting. I caught the guy at the door and said to him, "Wow, man, that was bold. You have a lot of boldness to do something like that." I think he was a bit confused, thinking that I would just tell him to leave and simply replied, "Thanks." I then said, "If I can speak into your life for a moment, I think that you're in fear because you were saying that as you were walking out of the room. You didn't choose to take a biblical stand, which would have been trying to go to your brother one-on-one. That would have taken more boldness than shouting and walking out."

You see, his approach to evangelism was the same: He was scared to take a stand and to see what would happen. Instead, he would yell and run. Sure, it looked bold, but the fruit was not there because the heart was not motivated by compassion or moving in love. Instead, the heart was filled with fear. Boldness void of compassion is a dangerous thing.

So what would boldness and compassion look like operating together?

One time our family was at Five Guys in Vancouver, Washington and Ellie, our oldest daughter, who was around 6 at the time, said, "Hey daddy, I think that we should tell all the people in here about Jesus." I agreed, so we got our food and when we were about to leave the restaurant we decided we'd stop at every table and share Jesus with them. The restaurant was full. After the first two tables, people in the restaurant noticed and began to wonder what was going on, because we were shifting the atmosphere with God's love.

That day, each and every table got a personal "Jesus loves you so much, is there any way we can pray for you today?" Not a scared individual working up the courage to yell at everybody before running away from them. Love will yield fruit because people respond to love.

Please make sure that your boldness is not just covered-up fear. Find the heart of God so that compassion becomes your strength.

Before You Approach Anyone, Have God's Heart For Them

It is so important to connect with God before engaging with people. Our motivation needs to be loving people. If we are not careful, we will go on outreach because we know that we are supposed to but our motivation will become, "I need to be going on outreach," rather than, "I desire to love people with God's heart."

The first time you step out, you are going to feel pressure and you might feel a bit awkward, you just have to press through that. Just make sure that you get God's heart before you do. If I'm about to go into a store with the family and I'm not really feeling all that motivated to love people and be a witness, I simply say, "God, please give me your heart for the people I encounter at this store." The moment that I reset my heart by asking for his heart, it becomes effortless.

It's Ok to Get a Word Wrong as Long as They Feel Loved

Oftentimes we are so worried about getting a word of knowledge wrong that we don't step out in faith and believe for God to come through. Words of knowledge and stepping out in faith are difficult things at times because you never really know if you're hearing correctly until you step out and ask. I have gotten so many words for people wrong and even today, after walking this lifestyle out for years, I still get words wrong. What I've learned is that if you lead with love in your heart towards the people that you are talking to, you will never be wrong. Love and a wrong word are better than the right word without love. People often won't remember if you got a wrong word, but they will almost always remember if they felt the love of Jesus as you spoke.

One time, when I was working as a construction worker and picking up supplies from Parr Lumber, I asked the man helping us load our vehicle, "Hey, do you have any pain in your knees?" He told me "No", but that his back had been really hurting him. I then asked him if I could pray for his back, to which he said, "Of course." At that moment, he was not one bit concerned about me getting the word of knowledge wrong, and neither was I because I got to love and to pray for him. If you are too concerned about getting the word right then it may actually be more about you than it is about honoring God with your faith and obedience. After I prayed a short, powerful prayer I asked how his back felt and he began to say, "It's hot, it's hot. My back is hot. What are you doing to me, are you a witch?" I was able to share with him that I'm a real Christian and that I love Jesus, and that Jesus was healing him.

It was powerful to see God move in such a powerful way. It didn't matter at that moment if I got the word right or wrong, what mattered was that I loved the man that I was talking to and I loved and honored God. And God moved because God can move if we move. We just need to have the right heart, His heart, when we do.

Often when I approach people with a word of knowledge, I'll say something like this, "Excuse me, sorry to bug you today, but I was walking by and I felt in my heart to ask you if you were having any trouble with your knees?" If they say, "No," then I simply say, "Is there anything that you do need prayer for?" More times than not they will say, "Yes" and begin to share with me their prayer needs. Sometimes when I get a word of knowledge wrong I will say something like, "I love practicing to hear God's voice. I don't always get it right but I love to lean in and listen to God the best I can." People always seem to appreciate the honesty and my hunger to connect with God.

My encouragement for you is to abide in the love of Christ and to be sensitive to how you communicate what you believe you're hearing and I believe you will begin to see great fruit and will really grow in the ability to hear and to respond to the voice of God.

You Are Not Selling God!
We Are Introducing Them to Our Friend, Jesus

When we share Jesus with people we are not trying to convince them to believe what we believe or trying to force or trick them into saying a prayer so that we can say somebody got saved. That wouldn't necessarily be someone getting saved as much as it would be pushing religion down their throat. Unfortunately, I have seen too many people go out and end up doing more damage than good when it comes to sharing the gospel because their approach is wrong.

We are not going out to sell something to someone or to convince somebody of something or to engage in a verbal debate. We are going out to introduce people to Jesus and his love. Salvation is a person and his name is Jesus. When we share with people about him, he comes and makes himself known in powerful ways to the people we are sharing with. It's our job to share in love and it's God's job to convince them that he is real and powerful to save. The moment that our evangelism shifts from preaching at people to sharing with people, things drastically change and you will see that in the fruit.

We have all seen the angry street preacher standing outside sporting events and concerts holding signs that say, "You're going to burn in hell." I have taken time to talk to these individuals who, more times than not, are really trying to honor God the best they can. When I talk to them I ask them if they have seen anybody won to the Lord in the past few years, more times than not, the answer is "No." It's sad because if they would put their energy towards loving people and proclaiming the real gospel, they would begin to see real fruit.

Before you begin to share with people, always remember that you don't need to force anything, you simply need to share with them about who Jesus is to you and who he wants to be for them. The gospel is always meant to be relational and never informational. If you can argue a person into praying a prayer and following Jesus, then somebody else can argue and convince a person not to follow Jesus. When a person has a true encounter with Jesus...well that is something that simply cannot be argued away.

People Are Not A Target

On outreach, people are often excited and a little nervous to get out there and share with people. It can be nerve-racking to step out and share with people at first. What I've learned is, if we're not careful, we can come off like we're targeting people because it's not something we naturally do all the time.

I have seen people go into grocery stores and appear to be stalking a person, just following them around the store, until they have the courage to talk to them. I have to be honest, to live a life of outreach you will definitely have to embrace the awkwardness and understand that we are different. That's okay, we're not called to look like the world. Embracing awkwardness and the fact that sharing Jesus with complete strangers is, in fact, different, can actually be a key to your success if you simply embrace it. And since that is true, we want to ensure that we don't make ourselves appear any weirder than we already are to the world!

When you step out and talk to people, it's important to be as normal and natural as you can be. I normally will say something like, "Hey, so sorry to bug you. I know your shopping but I wanted you to know that I'm a Christian and I love Jesus. Today I was praying and asking God to lead me to people to talk to and I really felt in my heart that he wanted me to talk to you." I believe in being totally honest and upfront with people from the beginning. If they want to talk, great. If not, I don't want to waste their time. People appreciate honesty and it makes the conversation so much easier because you're not trying to sneak Jesus in, you're letting them know he is the point.

One time I was in Walmart on outreach with a few friends and we approached a man near the bike section and said, "Hey man, we just spent time praying at our church and felt led to come to Walmart, and then when we saw you, and felt led to come and talk to you. Can we share the gospel and pray for you?" He said "Yes!" and was so blessed that God led us to him that day that he actually began to tear up. I knew that his heart was ready for the gospel. After sharing with him, he prayed to be born again and decided to follow Jesus. It was incredible. He didn't feel like a target of the outreach team, he felt loved and seen by God, and I know he felt respected by us being completely honest with him about why we were speaking to him. People can sense what is genuine and pure. Don't target them, just love them.

Be Encouraged, Everyone Starts Somewhere!
We Celebrate Where You Are At

One of my favorite outreach stories is from a lady that attended LCU when I pastored there. She was at a restaurant and saw a woman she felt in her heart she should talk to. She wanted to share Jesus with her but she was dealing with a lot of fear to step out that day. As she was trying to get the courage, she began to cry because she was struggling. As she was crying, she found the courage and began to walk towards the woman. When she got over to the woman, she was still crying and the woman looked at her and said, "Why are you crying?" Our student said, "I want to share about Jesus with you but I'm scared." The lady in return said, "I'm an atheist but go ahead and share, I will listen." Our student shared her testimony and the gospel with this woman. The woman didn't say yes to Jesus but she did listen intently. When they shared that testimony on the stage with all of us afterward, the auditorium erupted in celebration because somebody pushed through fear and shared Jesus anyway. That student changed from that moment on, she became bold. And I've also thought about that atheist who let her share. If she would have walked up confident, she may have been shut down. I believe God used those tears to soften that woman's heart. To prepare her heart to intently listen to the gospel that would be preached because someone was scared and did it anyway.

Until you go with the Gospel, you will never grow, and you will never truly know. Because she stepped out, she grew in God and she learned she could do it.

I want to encourage you to start today, no matter what it looks like, because you will never grow until you start. I'm good if you simply walk up to a person and say, "Jesus loves you," and walk away! I'm being a bit funny but at the same time, if you begin to be obedient to God and step out, you will grow. And I celebrate wherever you are today, and I can't wait to hear how much you have grown in days, weeks, months, and even years to come. Just start today!

Feedback is Healthy; Both Giving and Receiving

Feedback is healthy when it comes to outreach unless you're Jesus. Which, by the way, let's just settle that right here and now: you're not! What do I mean by healthy feedback? The truth is, we are all growing in sharing our faith and being more effective for the Kingdom. One of the greatest ways to grow is to ask people for feedback on what they experienced being on outreach with you. Even if the person is not as experienced as you in outreach, it's important to allow them to speak into your life. You don't have to take to heart all of the feedback but most of the time there are one or two things that a person will share that can really help an individual grow. Jesus sent them out two-by-two on purpose and for a purpose so that they could grow together. Oftentimes in an outreach setting, one person is likely to be bolder than another but that often means the other person is likely to be more sensitive to how the people are responding. It's important that the best qualities of both people come out, in which case iron sharpens iron. I have friends that help me often. When I get a little too bold or fired up they will oftentimes talk to me after an encounter and say something like, "Hey, that was awesome but next time maybe walk away," or "Hey, maybe just be a bit more relational." I always welcome that because I always want to grow and understand I cannot do that alone. I understand that the company around me can see things I cannot see, or help to sharpen me in ways I cannot sharpen myself. Learning to live with a heart that welcomes and celebrates healthy feedback will always yield growth.

I want to talk to pastors and outreach leaders for a moment. To the level that you empower somebody is the level that you need to confront that same person in love. Let's be honest, most people that show up for outreach are half-crazy, at least that's been my experience, and my wife and friends would tell you that I'm half-crazy as well!

Most of the people that will make up your outreach team or are on your outreach team already are hungry for feedback and are desiring to be fathered and mothered by people that genuinely care about them. So many times, I have seen that when I take the time to invest in individuals who are a part of our outreach team who are doing things wrong or have an approach to things that could shift, the conversation almost always goes great and that person feels loved and valued. As a byproduct, that individual will make the necessary changes and become even more effective in sharing their faith.

God tends to send me the people who have been misunderstood and, well for lack of better words, been removed from churches. What I believe happens is that these people have a genuine love for evangelism but have simply never been fathered. I genuinely believe that God sends them to churches to help bring in the lost but the pastors and leaders don't take the time to love and invest into them, which would help them grow. Instead, they've often let them exist within their community until people become so aggravated with their quarks that they're asked to leave, without ever telling them why. So many evangelists are walking around wounded by pastors and leaders who didn't choose to take the time to address the things that they needed to change in love. It's important to lead people with honor and honesty and it's important to take the time to invest in the people that God sends us.

There was a moment that really impacted me in this area and changed my perspective in a major way. I was on a trip with Evangelist Chris Overstreet in Prague, Czech Republic. We were sitting at a restaurant in the city square and a person ran up to the restaurant with a sign and began to shout about Jesus. It was not a good experience. It was not done in love. Once the man walked away, we all commented on what had happened and after we were all done giving our two cents, Chris Overstreet spoke up and said, "All that man needs is a father." Today, I can still hear those same words in my spirit. Oftentimes, people just need a father.

It's important to understand that we need to ask for feedback and give feedback in love. If you are talking to other people about the people you lead and work with but you are not talking to them personally, you are out of order. You need to share honestly with people, in love, and have the conversation needed, even if it's difficult. In doing so, you and that individual can both grow beyond where you are today.

Humility is Key; We Welcome Feedback and Lean Into It

Pride is a killer and the number one thing that it kills is your personal growth in the Kingdom. The Bible says that God resists the proud and gives grace to the humble. I want the grace of God in my life always, which means I need to have a heart that remains humble and low. One of the many ways that God tries to get our attention is by using those closest to us to speak into our lives. It's important to lean into those moments and welcome them, not run from them.

One day, Aaron Christopherson, the Co-founder of 33rd Company, called me and said he needed to talk to me. At the time he called me I was reading a book written by Bob Sorge Titled, "The Chastening of the Lord" (I highly recommend this book to you). As Aaron began to talk to me about a few different things, I knew in my heart that it was the Lord. He said all the right things on the phone but in my heart, I didn't want to receive it. It was hitting pride in my heart. I got off the phone and shared with my wife what the conversation was about, hoping that she would make me feel better. Her response was not what I wanted to hear, it was what I needed to hear. She began to tell me, in love, that she agreed and that those things in my life needed to shift. I can remember thinking and saying some pretty dumb things as I walked up the stairs to sulk and try to convince myself that I was right, so that I could remain in my pride. When I hit the top of the stairs I heard the Lord say, "You better listen, this is me and I'm saying these things to you because I love you." The Bible says that the Lord chastens the ones that he loves.

I decided to get over my pride and admit that I was wrong and I decided to change. I'm so glad that I listened because if I hadn't, I would have remained in pride and not grown to be a better man of God. When these moments of chastening come from people that you love and walk with, lean in and listen. Get over your pride. Choose humility. It will truly change the trajectory of your entire life.

OUTREACH | OUR APPROACH

Be Aware of Your Surroundings and How Others are Experiencing You

It's very important that we are aware of how people are experiencing us as we share Jesus with them. And not only the people that we are ministering to but the people that are around us as well. The more that we can honor people and our surroundings, the more fruitful we will be.

I share my faith everywhere I go. If I'm buying a coffee, I'm going to tell the barista that Jesus loves them. If I'm at the grocery store, the checkout clerk is going to hear the same thing. Because I'm sensitive and aware of the people around me, I also make sure not to be rude and rob people's time or hold up a line too long. If I'm at the grocery store, I will say something like, "Hey, I know that you are busy checking out all these customers and there is a line behind me, but as you ring up my groceries could I share my quick testimony with you?" If I'm at a sit-down restaurant I will say to the server something like, "Thank you so much for taking care of us today, we just want you to know that we love Jesus and that he loves you very much. Also, we know that you are very busy working so if you can think of anything that you might need prayer for before you bring us the food we would love to pray for you. And if you have two minutes for me to share the Gospel with you, I would love to share the Gospel with you." So often the server will bring the food to the table with a prayer request, and then we will ask, "Do you want us to pray for you standing here or would you rather us pray when you leave?" We want them to feel comfortable and like they have a choice, that's important. After we pray for them, they will normally come back to the table and say, "Okay, share with me, it's a busy night but I have two minutes for you to share with me." And then we take two minutes and share the gospel with them.

It's simple when we're honest and it's fruitful when we're aware of our surroundings and honor and respect people. Otherwise, we could really turn people off to the gospel by a lack of awareness. There is a balance to this thought however, because some may never think it's an appropriate time to share the gospel or it's not time because they feel uncomfortable. Listen, it's always time to share and it will almost always make people uncomfortable. What I'm trying to say is that you can do your best to make what can be an uncomfortable situation as normal as possible by moving in honesty, love, and awareness.

One night I was with my friend Jonnie at a Blazer game and he politely asked two young adult ladies that were working at an ice cream stand if he could share the gospel with them. There was nobody in line and the girls said, "Yes" so he very politely shared the gospel. As he was sharing, one of the girls began to get agitated and started to loudly shout at him, telling him to leave or she was going to call security. The other girl looked at me and asked if he was my friend. I said yes and joined the conversation, or at that moment, the one-sided shouting match. I calmly asked the girl who was upset if he had first asked her if he could share, to which she said, "Yes." I said, "Okay, and you're telling us now that you are done so we will leave but I want you to understand that in this situation you are the one with the problem. He politely asked you if he could share, you said 'yes', and you have nobody in line."

After my comments, she began to yell for security once again and we smiled and walked away. What was just a normal evangelism conversation turned into a demon manifesting through a woman that was not ready to say "Yes" to Jesus. When you share the gospel as much as Jonnie and I do, that happens sometimes. My encouragement to you is to be bold but also be aware, and always follow the Holy Spirit when you step out.

Be Relational When Approaching Others

When we are nervous and in a different situation than we'd normally find ourselves in, we tend to start acting a little bit different than we would if we were just going about our normal day. At the beginning, one of the hardest things for people going on outreach is deciding how to start the conversation. For that reason, I wanted to lay out a few ways that our team starts conversations with people. I believe these will help you get started but I want to encourage you to find out the most natural way to approach people for you, and do that instead of forcing something. That can take time to learn, to identify, and to grow in, so while you do, here are some ways you could begin conversations:

- "Sorry to bug you, but I was wondering if I could have 2 minutes of your time to share the gospel with you?"

- "Hi, my name is Chris. I just wanted you to know that Jesus loves you and I was wondering if you had one minute so I could share the gospel with you?"

- "Excuse me, sir, I just really felt led to stop and ask if I can pray for you?"

- "So sorry to stop you as you are walking into this store but our church, The Promise Church, is out at the moment sharing Jesus with people and asking if we can pray for them. Do you need prayer for anything or do you have a minute for me to share the gospel with you?"

- "Are you having a good day? I just wanted to let you know that Jesus loves you."

- "Excuse me, I was just walking by and felt in my heart that God wanted me to stop and ask if your back has any pain in it? If it does, I would love to pray for you!"

- "How are you? Is there anything you need prayer for?"

- "Jesus loves you. Is there any way I can pray for you today?"

Be Respectful of Other People's Time and Schedule

Have you ever been in a hurry to get somewhere and were running a bit behind? The red lights were just a little longer than normal or your wife is in the van with four kids and two of them are melting down? Sometimes time is not our friend. The people that you are talking to may be in a hurry and need to get somewhere. That is why it is so important on outreach to ask people if they have time, or tell them that you will only take a few minutes of their time to share with them. Most people have two minutes but very few have 10 minutes, unless they are hanging out at a park or on a walk. Most people are pretty busy and it's important to be aware of that and to respect that.

When we say "Share the gospel" to somebody, they probably have no grid for how long that will be. For all they know, they may be thinking, "Is this guy about to pull out his Bible and share the whole thing with me?" You can really put people at ease and get more people to listen if you simply add something about one or two minutes to what you say. Then, it's important to stay in the time frame you communicated. If the person seems really engaged, ask if you can have two more minutes. If the person is ready to hear the gospel they oftentimes will say, yes, and you can keep on sharing. I have won many people to the Lord in less than five minutes because they were ready, and because I have learned how to share the gospel in a way that is powerful and true in a very short amount of time.

If you are a person that struggles with time, take some time and practice sharing the gospel in two minutes with a friend or a family member. Learn to share your testimony in one minute. If you begin to honor people's time, you will begin to be more fruitful.

Outreaches are NOT Meant to Only Be Events; They are You Living Life Like Jesus

It's very important that outreach becomes a lifestyle of sharing Jesus with others, not an event. We call this being a full-time Christian. Oftentimes, the first time that somebody shares their faith is at an event of some sort with a group of people that are going out to share. I love evangelism events and I travel around the country and world speaking at them. I do this because I know that for many people, that event will be the starting point of a life spent sharing with others.

Before we go on outreach, we almost always take time to tell people to go and do the things that they would normally do, but as they go, to simply share Jesus with people. For example, if you like shoe shopping, go and shop for shoes and tell people about Jesus while you do it. It's very easy to fall into outreach mode and get very militant about what you are doing. We say all the time that if you are not having fun on outreach, you are doing it wrong. Why? Because we are at our best when we are relaxed and having fun.

One thing that I often do on outreach is go to Walmart and shop for my kids in the toy section. Maybe while I'm looking for a hot wheel that Noah doesn't have yet, I will run into somebody that needs Jesus. Also, when you are doing the things that you enjoy doing you will meet people who have the same interests as you and you will find it easy to talk with them. One way that we love to share our faith is after we play basketball. A group of my friends will go to the gym to play some pickup games and before we leave, we will ask all the guys if we can share with them. It's amazing to see how open people can become just after playing some basketball with them.

I want to encourage you to make your outreaches fun and full of the things that you love to do. If you do that, you will begin to find that sharing your faith comes easier when you're not on outreach. The goal of outreach events is to get people to share their faith while they go about their day. I would encourage you to make outreach like what you normally do day-to-day. This way, you can begin to do outreach every day as you simply live life. There are times that our Belong team goes on outreach for four to six hours in a day. If that's the case, we do different kinds of evangelism to break it up. We may start with door-to-door for two hours or go to 20 houses, then we will go to lunch and share with the people that we see there. Then, we will go out to shopping centers and coffee shops. If you have a longer time to go on outreach, break it up and keep it fresh and fun. That way, you will keep momentum. The main thing is that event evangelism needs to turn into full-time Christianity because ultimately, we are called to be full-time Christians who share our faith everywhere we go.

Pray Short Powerful Prayers

Whenever I ask to pray for somebody I always ask if I can pray a short, powerful prayer. Why do I say that? When you ask if you can pray for somebody that is not a Christian, they have no idea what prayer looks like or how long that prayer will be. They may think that you're going to pray for 10-15 minutes or more. Before I started asking this question, I would have people ask me how long it will take. That's why I began to share that it will be short. I say powerful so that it can build faith in them that God is going to show up for them. We don't need to draw out our prayers for people when on outreach, we can pray in short and effective ways that bring heaven to earth. I often pray no longer than 15-30 second prayers for people and then ask what they felt when I prayed. That gives me the ability to pray again if they are open to it and need it. Here is an example of short and powerful prayers:

One time I was at IKEA returning some furniture with my family in Portland, Oregon. I told a woman that Jesus loves her and that he had spoken to me about her back and shoulder while I was waiting in line. She said that she did have pain in her back and shoulders. When she said that all I said was, "Be healed in Jesus name." She looked at me as she felt the power of God come on her, and began to feel so much heat that she took her winter vest off and was totally and completely healed just at those simple words.

It's important we always remember prayer is not as much about what we say as it is about who we know. Jesus is the healer. If you are walking with him and in the Holy Spirit, your prayers will be effective. Pray short, powerful prayers that bring Heaven to earth.

When Praying for Healing Ask About Their Pain Level
Before and After Prayer

If you are praying for healing, it is very helpful to ask the person that you're praying for what their pain level is from 0-10. This gives you the opportunity to know if anything is shifting as you're praying. I have seen so many times people's pain go from an eight to a one or a zero after two or three prayers. If you pray and nothing seems to happen, ask the person for their contact information and let them know that you will continue to pray for them once you leave. When we pray, things happen. Even if we don't see it at the moment.

Years ago, Chelsea and I were at the mall in Vancouver, Washington and we stopped to pray for a woman that had a medical walking boot on her foot. We asked if we could pray and she agreed so we prayed and nothing seemed to change. We told her that we went to The Promise Church and that Jesus loved her, and then we kept shopping. Three months later, she called the church and was looking for the two young people that prayed for her at the mall that day. She told the church office that the moment that we walked away her foot became very hot and she took the boot off and her foot was totally healed. I would often think about that story and wonder why it happened that way, and today, I think I might know why it did. I believe God wanted us to know that he is God and that he heals people and we don't. We were young. We needed to be taught that it wasn't about us seeing it, it was about God doing it.

Lead with the Gospel! Make Sure When Praying for the Sick That You Share the Gospel with Them as Well

We love praying for the sick and seeing people healed. We pray for the sick daily and know that it is something that God has called us to do as believers. More importantly, we share the gospel with people we encounter. A healed knee doesn't change somebody's eternity, salvation through Jesus does. In order for people to receive salvation, they need to hear the gospel. We say this often, "We don't want somebody with a healed knee to keep walking towards hell." The gospel needs to be shared. I know that healing is exciting and actually, in most circumstances, a little bit less intimidating than sharing the gospel. Most people are open to prayer when they are sick but not all people are open to the gospel. It becomes fairly easy to approach people and say, "Can I pray for you?" You can actually do that and never mention the name of Jesus. But the moment that you bring in the gospel and Jesus, things can shift and change in a moment. Things can shift eternally.

It's important that we share the gospel because the gospel is the power of God unto salvation. If you go out to encourage people, people will be encouraged. If you go out to pray for people, people will encounter the love of God and oftentimes be healed and encouraged by your prayers. But if you go out to share the gospel, people will be saved.

So how can you lead with the gospel on outreach? It really is quite simple, just start with mentioning the gospel somewhere in the conversation.

The other day I was at the mall with my family heading to a video arcade. I stopped to talk to two young men who were sitting at a table eating dinner. I started the conversation by saying, "Hey guys, my name is Chris, and I really felt led to tell you that Jesus loves you very much." They said, "Thank you," and my next statement was, "Are you guys believers in Jesus?" One of the young men said, "Yes," and the other said that he was open to the idea and that he was on a journey listening to other people's ideas. I said, "Okay, well I'm about to go to the arcade with my family but before I go, could I take a minute to share the gospel with you?" What was interesting was the one young man who was a believer said, "No." I said to him, "Well, I'm not talking to you, I'm talking to your friend and if you were a real believer you would say, 'Yes'." I then shared with the young man who was open to the simple gospel. It was nothing complicated at all. I knew that I was simply sowing seeds into his heart. He gave me a fist bump and I walked away. This is an example of how you lead with the gospel.

One of the reasons that people don't share the gospel when they are on outreach is because they don't know how to articulate the gospel in a simple way. There are many different, great tools out there to help you share the gospel. I would encourage you to find a way to share that is short and powerful and can become natural, and then learn to lead with the gospel. The reason why we don't see more people saved on outreaches is not complicated. It is because we don't share the gospel. If you share the gospel, people will be saved. Learn to love the gospel and begin to share it with people and you will begin to see people come to Christ more often.

The Gospel is Enough!

Oftentimes when outreaches happen people have a tendency to look for physical needs that they can meet, and then they share the gospel with the person that they helped. This is a great form of evangelism. I am all for this and do this often. We can take food to the poor and homeless or give away school supplies to families that could use the help financially. We can offer free food and fun activities for families that can't afford to take their family to a place of entertainment. We can also go on outreach and look for people that need prayer for healing, and when we find a person, run up to them and pray for them. That is great. I stop and pray for many of the injured and sick people that I see at airports, parks, and malls. All of these things are great and we should do all of them often. But I do want to share a perspective with you that I believe can help remind us that all people who don't have Jesus are in great need.

In the Bible, Jesus called all different kinds of people to follow him, those who were demonized and set free, those who were dead and raised up, and those who sat in a tax collecting booth with lots of money and power. What I'm trying my best to communicate to you is that the guy in the red sports car with a million-plus dollars in his bank account is just as bankrupt as the guy living on the side of the street if he doesn't have Jesus. Without Jesus, he is spiritually dead and desperately needs the life of Christ in his life.

If our evangelism only focuses on the ones who are in physical need, then we are missing sharing the gospel with the larger part of America. Jesus had the ability to see the crowd as they really were. A crowd is made up of many different kinds of people. In Matthew 9:36 ESV it states, "When he saw the crowds, he had compassion for them, because they were harassed and helpless, like sheep without a shepherd." We need to pray to have the ability to see the crowd the same way that Jesus does. When we do, we can be moved by compassion to reach out to all people around us, despite their material status or physical appearance. A soul without Jesus is a soul who needs Jesus, period.

I understand that for some reason it can feel more intimidating to talk to people who don't have an obvious physical need. I have experienced this. What I do is, I simply remind myself that they are in need of Jesus and that that is the greatest need that person can have. Then, I remind myself that the gospel is enough. What do I mean by that statement? I mean sometimes we can fall to the lie that we need healing or giving in order to open the door to share the gospel but what I have found is that sharing the gospel alone is more than enough. Choose not to be intimidated. Pray and ask to see people as they really are without Jesus, and then step out and share your testimony and the simple gospel with them. You will see lives transformed as you go with the gospel because the gospel is enough.

OUTREACH | FOLLOW UP

It Doesn't Cost You Your Life to Preach the Gospel, It Does Cost You Your Life to Disciple Others

You can go out on outreach for a few hours and check that box off and then go back to life as normal. You can do this and not steward the people that God put in your path on the outreach. It may cost you some of your time to go out and share the gospel but when you begin to invest your life into the people that get saved, it begins to cost you your life.

When I say cost you your life what I mean is, it will cost you changing the way that you live your life today. Your lifestyle will have to change and, for some, you're very comfortable and that's hard.

After God spoke to me in the dream about creating a net for him to fill, Chelsea and I talked about what that would look like for a few weeks. We knew what God was asking us to do, and if we were going to obey him, we were going to have to give up a night of the week to disciple new believers. It took us a few weeks of thinking about it, and then we decided on Tuesday at 6:30 PM. After we made a decision that was not easy, we began to experience the joy of discipleship like we never had before and the cost that was associated with it at the beginning seemed to disappear. That night of the week became one of our favorite nights of seeing people's lives transformed. I remember when that night of the week became too full of people and we started talking about a second night of the week. That was another couple of weeks of us talking and praying about what we were going to do, and then we gave another night a week to discipleship. Again, it was amazing what God would do with our obedience. At times, we would feel the cost but being able to witness lives change was so amazing that we got to learn first-hand that it's worth it. Discipleship will cost you your time, your comfortability, your routine, and your life – and it will be worth it.

I have talked to pastors and leaders about Belong and discipleship and their response is often excitement. Most of the time when I talk to people they become very interested in starting one themselves. Then, a few months go by and they end up not doing it. I think one of the main reasons why they don't end up doing it is because the cost of change is too much. In order to get different fruit, you have to do things differently. There are many wonderful churches out there that are not seeing people saved and discipled. What I want to help people see is that you can keep having your wonderful church and doing the same things that you have been doing for years that you have grown to love and enjoy, there just needs to be a shift. A shift that will help bring in the lost to see people saved and discipled. My encouragement is if you have a heart to win people to the Lord and to disciple people, and that is not happening regularly at your church, then change what you are doing so that you can have different fruit. Count the cost of discipleship and make the shift now because when you do it, you will not regret it one bit.

You Can't Separate Evangelism from Discipleship

You can't have discipleship without evangelism, because you will have nobody to disciple, and outreach without discipleship is very shallow. Jesus said, "Go and make disciples," not, "Go and tell people about me and leave them to figure it out on their own."

Evangelism and discipleship have been completely separated in the west. We have discipleship pastors and evangelism directors, and most of the time the discipleship pastors are focused on one half of their job, which is helping the church grow. This is great but it often means no new believers are being discipled, and the outreach director becomes consumed with running and planning events. I'm all for events but an evangelism director or pastor's main job description should not be organizing an Easter egg hunt or Christmas present giveaway, they should be equipping the church to win the lost and make disciples. I actually believe that the role should be the same person and was never meant to be a pastor or a director but a five-fold evangelist. The church at large knows that they are called to take the gospel to their community and to the world. What I have often seen happen is that a church hires a good administrative-minded person to plan and run evangelism events throughout the year so that the church can say that they are engaging the world with the gospel and being a light. I will never say anything negative about anything that a church does to bless the community and mission field but when these events lack an actual evangelist leading them or speaking into them, they result in acts of kindness without the gospel being shared at all. The church and its leaders may convince themselves that they did something great because they put resources towards blessing the community but did it accomplish our job as the church? Did the gospel go forward? Were the lost saved and plugged into community to be discipled?

Again, I'm all for blessing the community but what happens at these events is we fail to do the very thing that we are called to do. Why is there a lack of sharing the gospel? Because the people leading the events are not equipped or called as a five-fold minister of the gospel. Oftentimes they are actually ignorant to the fact that they should share the gospel with people, or they are scared. So the church instead takes the approach of, "If we bless them with stuff maybe they will come to church." Let's be honest, giving away free stuff will never make disciples. Preaching the gospel and people choosing to follow Jesus will.

There was a time that a friend of mine was on a mission trip and was sharing the gospel with people that she came in contact with throughout the day. One day, as the team was getting food, she began to share the gospel with the people at the food stand. One of the people that was working gave their life to Jesus and was born again right there. Then, one of the leaders of the mission trip who was from another church talked to her later and said, "We don't do that on these trips, we just love people." When I heard about this, I was pretty upset to think that a leader of a mission trip would say, "We don't preach the gospel and make disciples, we just love people." Actually, what the leader was saying is, "I don't ever do this because it makes me uncomfortable and it convicts me, so you shouldn't do it either so that I can feel better about coming on a mission trip and not share the gospel."

You see, the sad thing is that there are many outreaches and mission trips that occur that are full of people who never share the gospel and never intend on sharing the gospel. To me, that is a great problem that needs to be changed within the church. We actually need to share the gospel and make disciples. And that is the best way to love all people.

Connect With People Outside of a Church Setting

If a person is not able to make it to your Belong gathering and works on Sunday morning, then we make time to connect with that person during the week. We can tend to forget that people we meet and invite have no grid for church or church events. For us, it is something that is built into our life and our schedule. We do church because that's what we do. Sunday is church day, Wednesday is youth night, and every other Friday is young adults (or something like that). People that get saved don't have a church schedule all figured out and, oftentimes, work during our church meeting times. It's important that you are open to connecting at times that are convenient for those that get saved, even if it is not the most convenient for you. Remember, it often won't cost you your life to preach the gospel but it will cost you your life to make disciples.

There was a man who was truly born again when I was in Tampa, Florida. He was a barber. I reached out to him many times to invite him to church, Belong, and even lunch when it worked for him. It never seemed like he had time. He would always get back to me but he was always busy. I believed he genuinely wanted to connect and just truly didn't have the time, and I've found that to be true of many people. In response, I decided to change my barber. He became my new barber instead because that way I could spend time with him and disciple him. I was willing to shift my life to meet him where he was and I think it's important we always remain willing to do just that. Discipleship costs us convenience. It costs us our life, and like we always say, it's not always glamorous but it is absolutely glorious.

Ask For Their Name and a Way to Connect with Them If It Seems Appropriate

On outreach, it's important to understand that you are going to talk to many people and, in many cases, you are going to be sowing seeds of the gospel into people's hearts and giving them a church invite card, Belong invite card, or simply inviting them to come. We create door hangers that we take door-to-door that are a very effective way to invite people and get them the necessary information. We have seen Christians respond who just moved to the area and are looking for a church or are looking to get back into church because they have fallen away. When it comes to people that are making a first-time decision to follow Jesus, it is a bit different. We have found that handing them a card and inviting them is not enough to get them to walk through the doors of the church or Belong gathering. If a person made a genuine decision to be born again and follow Jesus, however, we have found that they are almost always open to giving you their phone number or connecting with you on social media.

If I'm on outreach and end up leading a woman to the Lord, I oftentimes ask them if can I get their number so that I can connect them with one of the ladies on our team that will reach out to them, or other times I may tell them that my wife Chelsea will reach out to them. It just depends on where I'm at and who I'm working with at that given time. During my time at LCU, I started a "Know their name campaign," which was so fun to see the shift in the student body.

Oftentimes if we are not careful, outreach time can become, "Go and get a testimony time." This is great because we should all have testimonies from what God is doing in and through our lives but if we're not careful, we can be so excited that God did something through us that we don't think to even know or get the person's name that Jesus was trying to reach through us. An outreach that is meant to be all about reaching others can actually in the end become all about us without even realizing it.

When we began to ask the students to remember the names of the people they met on outreach, something shifted. The focus of the outreaches and the testimonies became about the person that God touched, not the students that went out. When you remember the names of the people you connect with, it also gives you the ability to pray for them. I write down the names of people and where I meet them in my phone. That way, I can remember who they were, what God did, and how I can pray be praying for them. I think it's important for all of us to be a part of the, "Know their name campaign." It will help keep our hearts right. It will help us hold the heart of Jesus, never making it about ourselves but always keeping it about the one.

Be Consistent in Reaching Out to People That You Meet and Create a Discipleship List

One thing that our team does is something that Evangelist Scott McNamara with Jesus at the Door taught me, and that is creating a discipleship list that helps keep track of all the people that we meet throughout the day and on outreaches. This is a simple, very practical step that helps keep things organized so we can reach out to them. I keep this list in my phone notes. Then, I set aside time in my calendar to reach out to the people on my discipleship list and invite them to church and to Belong. I find that if I don't set aside time in my week to reach out to them, then I don't do it. I actually put the time in my calendar to do this, and then at that time, I reach out and invite everybody to church and Belong for that week. I will then send a reminder out to our team that is working with us to do the same thing as well.

We have found that it may take a few weeks or even months until a person comes. This is why consistency is key in this process. In Florida, after Rashad was saved outside the restaurant that he works at, it took six weeks before he ever came to church. That was six weeks of reaching out and inviting him, sometimes with no response. However, this was vital in getting him there. It's important to know that sometimes people will never respond, even after they have a powerful encounter with the Lord. We have come to a place where we expect this and choose not to be discouraged by it. We must choose to press on and keep inviting people to join us with great consistency because as we do, it begins to happen. People begin to come. I've seen it time and time again.

The people who don't write or call us back we believe had an encounter with God that marked them, and we pray they find a church and people to connect with in the future. Again, it's important to remember the pressure is not on us. God said, "Create a net and he will fill it." We simply ready ourselves to walk with the ones that he sends us who are ready to be discipled, and he has been so faithful to send them.

SECTION 4:
DISCIPLESHIP IS FAMILY

After I gave my life to Jesus when I was 18 years old, my hand was stuck to a Bible, and I was delivered from demonic bondage and I began to attend The Promise Church.

Casey Schang, who has been my friend since third grade, was the pastor's son. Scott and Lori Schang were the Senior Pastors and over the years, when I would stay at Casey's house on a Saturday night, I would go to church with him on Sunday morning. When I went to church with him, it was a different experience than what I was used to. At that time, my parents went to a conservative church that had traditional music out of hymn books accompanied by a piano. I never had a bad experience at Casey's church. I think back to these times and can remember liking the experience a lot. When I got older, I would hear people talk about The Promise Church in a negative way because they spoke in tongues and believed in the supernatural. And I'm sure glad they did speak in tongues and believe in the power of God because they were used by God to help set me free.

On the night of the greatest need of my life for freedom, my parents called Casey's dad, Scott. We had a relationship with them and my parents knew that he believed in the power of God. Scott and Lori came to pray for me that night, and I got completely delivered.

Having known Casey pretty much my entire life, he is more like a brother to me than a friend. When I got saved and filled with the Holy Spirit, Casey was there. He discipled me the most on my journey of discovering the Kingdom of God. At that time, I didn't even know what discipleship was. To me, Casey was the friend that I grew up with and enjoyed hanging out with. When I got saved, I continued hanging out with him but my eyes were opened to see that Casey loved God and knew him in a way that I didn't, but wanted to. After I got saved, there was a season that I was with Casey nearly every day. It was a wild time and I needed community because the devil didn't want to let me go easily. I would wake up in the night and have demons attacking me or while I was driving, the enemy would come and bring fear and try to intimidate me. In those moments, I would call Casey or just sleep at his apartment. Casey was a big help and strength to me in that season, and he was used by God to help me navigate a lot and to teach me how to be a Christian. We didn't do any formal bible studies or official discipleship classes. He didn't walk around and tell people that I was his disciple and that he was helping me. He was just simply my friend that was further along on his journey with God than I was, and he helped me get to know God better.

When I joined The Promise Church, I met many more people of all ages who began to pour into my life and help me grow in God. Jonathan, Aaron, Pastor Kevin, and many more people began to come around me and love me and help me on my journey. The Promise Church became my family. I wasn't just going to church on Sunday morning, I was doing life with these people every day and, in doing life with them, I was being discipled without even really knowing that's what it's called.

To me, this is what discipleship is meant to be. I know that it won't always be like my story, but I do believe that discipleship was never meant to be a program, it was always meant to be family. People know when they are in a program or process and we are just trying to move them onto the next step in the process. They also know when they are in a real family that loves them and cares about them. I'm not against programs or processes at all, Belong is a program of sorts to help churches effectively step into winning the lost and discipling new believers. But it's important that it is about the relationship with the people that God sends you over the process and program that you're trying to set up. Programs don't excite me, they never will. What wakes me up in the morning is knowing that people I'm walking with, who were once lost, are connecting with God and coming to life.

After I got saved in the way that I did, I couldn't be quiet about what happened to me, so I would share with people often about what God did in my life. I got saved a year after I graduated high school, so many of the people that I went to school with were still in town and around the area. I would run into them and have the ability to share with them what happened to me, if they hadn't already heard about it. Woodland is a pretty small town, the kind of place where, if you're just going to the grocery store, you're probably going to see at least one or two people that you know.

About a year after I was saved, I ran into a guy that went to Woodland High School with me. He was in my class and ran on the cross country team. I'm going to call him Charles in this story. In high school, Charles was not a cool kid. In fact, he was the exact opposite of that, he was the kid that many made fun of. He had long hair and he didn't bathe. His skin was completely covered with acne and he smelled bad (I'm sure you can imagine the smell of somebody that didn't take a shower). Later on, Charles told me that he didn't take a shower at home because the shower was too small and the shower head was too low, so he didn't think that he could take a proper shower so he never attempted to.

When I reconnected with him after high school, I befriended him and asked him to come along to different church gatherings and functions that were happening. We had a very lively youth group with a lot of things going on and a lot of friends doing stuff at all times. A few weeks into reconnecting with him, Charles gave his life to Jesus, and slowly he began to change. For a season, I did life with Charles. I would hang out with him every day after work, and a few weeks after being saved, he was filled with the Holy Spirit and began to speak in tongues. After a month or so, we began to ask him if we could help him with his hygiene. He was slow to allow us to help him because for years he was made fun of but God was moving in his life and he was slowly being opened to it. We started by convincing him to take a shower. The first shower that he took in, who knows how long, was at my parent's house. Then, he cut his fingernails (they were super long). After that, we started talking about cutting his hair. The first time we took him to get his haircut it was all the way down his back and he cut off approximately two inches. We were thinking a full-on haircut was going to happen and that would have been nice but we were taking baby steps. We then got everybody to pitch in and gathered close to $300 dollars together, which back in the day was big money to us, so that we could take him shopping and get him some new clothes. We even had a woman at the church stop us on a Sunday and say, "Hey, I want to give you some money to help Charles, what you guys are doing for him is amazing." She gave me a hundred-dollar bill to help, so we took him shopping with all the money we had gathered. About 6 months later, he looked like a completely different person. His skin had cleared up, he was clean, and he looked good. He also ended up going into the military, which was a big surprise to many because that would not have been an option in school. In high school, he would finish last if he even finished any cross country race at all. We were all watching the outside transform, and it was happening because his heart was transforming at the very same time.

At the time, I didn't know that what we were doing was called discipleship, but it was. Charles's life, and mine, would be totally changed after that season. Because when you disciple somebody, it doesn't just change them. It changes you in an amazing way. It changes you because you get to witness firsthand the power of God transforming a person's life. Charles was the first person that I got to love and disciple as Casey loved and discipled me. And it has marked me to this day.

A few months after Charles went into the military, God brought me another person to walk with. I will call him Tim. Tim was my age and his family attended my church but he and his brothers did not. Tim was addicted to drugs and in a tough spot when I connected with him and began to disciple him. It's important to understand that I began to hang out with him before he was saved. Oftentimes, we only have relationships with people that know God and that needs to change. Tim was saved and filled with the Holy Spirit in my parent's basement. I can remember praying for him to receive the Holy Spirit, and when we prayed, I watched as a demon came out of him and he felt the presence of God come into him. I walked upstairs for a moment and when I came back down, he was sitting there praying in the Holy Spirit. About a week later, I was over at his apartment and there was a knock on the door. When he went to answer it, there was a man standing there that had acid scars on his face where somebody threw acid on him and it permanently scarred his face. I was still a fairly new believer, so I was a bit uncomfortable when the man came in and sat down on the couch next to me. He was telling Tim that he owed him money and Tim was promising to get it to him. As the conversation continued, I noticed that the man kept moving further and further away on the couch from me until he was backed into the corner of the couch and finally said, "Who is this guy? He is freaking me out. There is a bright light and I feel power coming off of him." I told him who I was and then was able to share my testimony with him. It was amazing. Me being there that night helped that situation go much smoother than it would have gone had I not been there. I was just a young, 19-year-old Christian that was filled with the Holy Spirit, and I was scaring a grown man coming to collect drug money.

After this encounter, I actually had a season of walking with that man. He never accepted Christ but he had a lot of seeds planted in his heart. Tim's life was headed in the right direction but he could no longer sell drugs to make a living, so we needed to find him a job. At the time, I worked at a feed store in town with my friend James. We had done such a good job running the store that the owner was happy to hire Tim. So Tim began to work with us and we discipled him as we did life together. Tim became a brother in my life that I loved dearly. He was working with me, and my parents even took him in. He tried to run from the Lord for a short season but God ultimately won and Tim is still following the Lord today. Discipleship with Tim was more than taking him to church on Sunday, it was investing into his life and loving him along his journey. I didn't have a Belong to take him to, so I took him to my parent's house.

Discipleship is helping people grow in God and helping people out in life. We got him a place to stay, we got him a job, and we became his friends. To this day, when I'm back in my city and I see him, he has a deep level of gratitude for me because I invested time into his life and he is serving God today because of the grace of God and the love that I, and many others, have shown him.

When I was in Florida pioneering the Belong at Generation Church, I had the honor of making many new friends. I can remember before I got to Florida I would often think, "I wonder who I will lead to the Lord? Who is it that will be added to my life and my family?" God added some pretty amazing people into my life that have become like family to me. I will never forget the day that I met Frank and Kyle at their house when we were going door-to-door. That day, meeting them changed their life but it also changed mine. I have learned that people are the true treasure that God gives us. Those two men have become brothers in my life that I love dearly.

I can remember meeting Rashad one day on outreach, and seeing him six weeks later when he came to church for the first time. The last official Belong that I was at in Florida, Rashad was water baptized and filled with the Holy Spirit. I couldn't help but cry because he was what I moved my family to Florida for. I went to Florida to make disciples, and Rashad was one of those disciples that God filled our net with. And beyond getting to disciple him, I have a deep love for him.

Then there is Teddy, the cafe owner that became so dear to me. I met him one day while I was meeting Kyle and Frank for coffee. One of the best discipleship moments was going to his cafe one day for lunch and spending time talking and building a friendship with him after he had a radical encounter with God. On my last Sunday in Florida, I got to baptize Teddy in the church lobby with a small crowd of people around. He added to my life and makes it better.

You see, what I have learned in these past few years is that we are not trying to conquer the world, we are trying to make disciples. And I have learned that when we make disciples, it enriches our life as much as it enriches theirs. My hope is that I can get the young evangelists that are coming up in the ranks to think about the names of the people that they are going to win to the Lord, not the names of the stadiums that they hope to fill. It's all about the one. It's all about the people that God sends you to walk with and to help along their journey in God.

My prayer has become, "Lord, give me another Frank who is ready for you. Give me another Kyle who is searching for you. Give me another Jason that is losing his family and needs you. Give me another Rashad that is lost without you. Give me another Ni'am that needs an encounter with you."

My prayer is that God will fill my net with people that are ready for him. This is my goal, that I can have just one more person added to my life.

As I write this, I'm on a plane flying from Dallas, Texas to Portland, Oregon, about to embark on pioneering another Belong in the months to come. As I write this, I can't help but cry thinking about the people that I have in my life but also thinking about the people that God will add. I believe this is the heart of God. This is what he wants us to be focused on, and if we focus on making disciples, he will focus on building the church, filling stadiums, and starting ministries. And then he will be able to entrust us with those churches, stadiums, and ministries because our hearts are pure and focused on the right thing. They're focused on the one. We can never forget that Jesus left the 99 for the one. Will you consider leaving the business of life and ministry for the one? What if this year you discipled one person? I promise you, it would completely change your life.

I can't think of a better last story that I could end on than Joel's story. Joel is a true friend and a brother that my family is committed to. He has made my life better and richer. I have seen a lot of transformations in people's lives but Joel's story will always stand out to me as one of the most powerful transformations I've gotten the privilege of witnessing. He not only loves God, he loves God and tells the world about him daily. I actually think it would be best to have Joel share his story with you:

I was born again in a Baptist church in Longview, Washington on June 5th, 2016. After attending a few services, God spoke to me and told me to go to the Promise Church in Woodland, Washington where I would meet Pastor Chris Donald. Just freshly surrendering my life to Christ, I was extremely hungry and fervently seeking truth. I was coming out of a long battle of about 18 years of addiction from alcohol, tobacco, and drugs. I suffered for much of my life from depression, bipolar mood disorder, and anxiety attacks and was on a high dose of antidepressants. Mentally, I was all over the place. I had a lot of zeal but little wisdom and understanding of my new faith.

After a Sunday service and chat with Chris, we decided to set up a meeting to walk through deliverance and help me understand the gospel. I remember the day vividly. I came to the church to meet

Chris and I had been going through a very crazy time since giving my life to Jesus. Mentally, physically, and spiritually I was out of my mind.

I remember walking up to Chris in the hallway right outside of the offices and looking into his piercing blue eyes, I saw hope. For the first time, I had peace that everything was going to be okay. It's all I wanted. The battle inside was fierce but I had faith for victory. I had real hope for the first time in my life. During the meeting, Chris explained the gospel and laid his hands on me. He cast out every tormenting devil. I won't go into great details but there were many. The chaos in my mind vanished. I instantly felt free.

Leading up to this, I had been battling serious anger and rage outbursts, tormenting thoughts of death, suicide, intense terror, anxiety attacks, and fear. I had an addiction to several substances and over-the-counter prescriptions. Within two months of my deliverance meeting, I was completely free of all substances. Tobacco, alcohol, and at the time cannabis dependency. I quit taking my antidepressant medicine because I didn't need it. I was free and I believed it! Whom the Son sets free is free indeed! That day, Chris called my mom to tell her everything was going to be okay. He told her that I was going to make it! That day, Chris told me there would be a process I would walk through to receive even more freedom, and that I needed to read my Bible every day and give God my whole life. I remember saying, "Yes, that's all I want!"

I left that meeting that day so much more hungry for God and for truth. I began to read the Bible every day for several hours. Sometimes up to six hours because all I wanted was the truth. All

I could do was read the word, worship, and pray. I didn't leave my bedroom all summer except to go to church on Sunday. No joke!

Chris then (shortly after our meeting) prayed for me to receive the baptism in the Holy Spirit. I received my prayer language that day and we began to meet weekly. Chris instantly began to disciple me one-on-one. Matthew 28:19-20. As I read through the gospels, I read about baptism. I instantly wanted to be baptized and began to mention it to Chris. On August 21, 2016 after Sunday service Chris, David Vahndijk, Joel Fenter (the guy who led me to Jesus), my family and a few others met me at Horseshoe Lake in Woodland and Chris water baptized me. It was powerful! I may have went down in water but I came up with fire!

Chris would begin to invite me up to his house to spend time with him and his family. I quickly fell in love with his whole family! In too many ways to mention, the Donald family has shown me God's amazing love. Chris showed me that discipleship is family, and for a short time in Texas, I even lived with the Donald's. He says it doesn't cost you your life to preach the gospel but it will cost you your life to make disciples. Chris has invested a lot of time into my life and has stood by my side for the last five years. He encouraged me through many difficult times. My life has been radically transformed by God's grace and mercy. Without discipleship, I highly doubt I would be who I am today. Every step of the way I was pointed to Jesus and given an example of what it looks like to be a disciple of Jesus Christ.

Today, everywhere I go I share the gospel, seeing God heal, deliver and save. From grocery stores, malls, restaurants, coffee shops, and anywhere else my feet take me, the power of the gospel is shared and demonstrated.

Chris has shown me the importance of being led by compassion and by the Holy Spirit. I am so thankful for Chris, Chelsea, & the entire Donald family.

- Joel Anthony Loveall

Discipleship, I believe, is meant to be family.

We in the western church need to begin to position our hearts and homes to receive the harvest that is coming in. I have heard many people get excited about the billion soul harvest that many prophets have prophesied is coming soon. I have been around many Christians and leaders who talk about the massive group of people that will be added to the Kingdom of God. I have been at church gatherings and conferences when people get excited about what is going to come. I'm excited about what is coming in the future as well but if I'm honest, I'm a bit overwhelmed thinking about all those people that will be coming into the Kingdom that will be needing a family of believers to walk with them like Casey did with me. And like I did with the people that I have shared about in this section. This concern that I began to feel a few years ago, I believe, was the Lord showing me that I needed to shift. I began to seek God for his heart and He then gave me the blueprint for Belong. He spoke to me about his heart for discipleship because my heart began to be greatly burdened by what his heart is all about. I was burdened about what it would be like to have all these people added to the church. I was burdened for the lost. I began to see and understand that we have to make a shift in order to see many added to the church.

Belong, I believe, is one of God's heavenly strategies for the end-time harvests. I believe that many people will be saved through this ministry in the next decade of harvest that is coming. It's going to be large and God is looking for laborers. And I want to encourage you, don't be overwhelmed with the task at hand, just simply start today. God will give you his grace to see many saved and discipled as you simply love the people in front of you today. And then do it again tomorrow, too.

It's not complicated. It simply takes creating a net so that God can fill it. He will be faithful to fill it with people who desperately need to be added to our Kingdom family. Discipleship looks like having somebody over for dinner, playing basketball with friends, going to lunch after church, watching a football game, going for a walk, playing catch in the street, helping a person get a job, or putting together money to buy new clothes for somebody in need. It's not complicated, it's just love. Love that demands a shift from the normal routines of life. Love that is fueled by and burdened for the things Jesus cares about most. Love that is willing to be inconvenienced. Because remember, it doesn't cost you your life to preach the gospel but it will cost you your life to make disciples. It's not always going to be glamorous but it is going to be glorious.

NOW GO! GO AND MAKE DISCIPLES!

"Therefore go and make disciples of all nations, baptizing them in the name of the Father and of the Son and of the Holy Spirit, and teaching them to obey everything I have commanded you. And surely I am with you always, to the very end of the age."

- Matthew 28:19-20

SECTION 5:
BELONG MULTIPLICATION

Our team has everything needed to equip you to begin! I want to encourage you, however big or small that start may be, just start. I believe you will be amazed by how Jesus partners with and lands on your obedience to respond to the call, because remember...the original call never changed!

Simply scan this code to visit our website to get started.

A GOD-GIVEN BLUEPRINT
TO CONTINUALLY REACH THE LOST
& DISCIPLE NEW BELIEVERS

PRAYER | OUTREACH | DISCIPLESHIP

CONVERSATION STARTER

HELLO MY NAME IS _____, I'M OUT TODAY LOOKING TO SHARE THE GOSPEL WITH PEOPLE. WOULD YOU HAVE 2 MINUTES FOR ME TO SHARE THE GOSPEL WITH YOU?

HELLO MY NAME IS _____, WE JUST SPENT TIME PRAYING AT OUR CHURCH AND ARE NOW OUT LOOKING TO PRAY FOR PEOPLE AND SHARE THE GOSPEL WITH PEOPLE. DO YOU HAVE A MINUTE FOR ME TO SHARE WITH YOU?

HEY, I WANT YOU TO KNOW THAT JESUS LOVES YOU. CAN I PRAY FOR YOU IN ANY WAY?

TWO ENGAGING QUESTIONS

1. DO YOU BELIEVE THAT GOD CREATED YOU TO BE IN A RELATIONSHIP WITH YOU?
2. DO YOU BELIEVE THAT SIN HAS MESSED THAT RELATIONSHIP UP?

GOSPEL STATEMENT

JESUS IS THE ANSWER TO THE SIN PROBLEM, HE CAME FROM HEAVEN TO EARTH TO MAKE A WAY FOR YOU TO COME INTO RELATIONSHIP WITH GOD.

DECISION

DO YOU WANT TO MAKE A DECISION TO FOLLOW JESUS TODAY AND TO BE BORN AGAIN?
IT'S IMPORTANT TO UNDERSTAND THAT SALVATION IS NOT ONLY A PRAYER. IT'S COMING INTO A RELATION-SHIP WITH JESUS AND FOLLOWING HIM FOR THE REST OF YOUR LIFE.

JOHN 17:3 NKJV
"AND THIS IS ETERNAL LIFE, THAT THEY MAY KNOW YOU, THE ONLY TRUE GOD, AND JESUS CHRIST WHOM YOU HAVE SENT."

FOLLOW US ON SOCIAL MEDIA

@33RDCOMPANY

INSTAGRAM | FACEBOOK | YOUTUBE

THIRTY THIRD COMPANY
MAKE DISCIPLES
THE ORIGINAL CALL NEVER CHANGED
33
WWW.33RDCOMPANY.ORG

NOW
GO!
& O.
MAKE
DISCIPLES
33RDCOMPANY.ORG